Te Kīngitanga

Te Arikinui Dame Te Ātairangikaahu, the Māori Queen.

Te Kīngitanga

The People of the Māori King Movement

Essays from
The Dictionary of New Zealand Biography

Foreword by Sir Robert Te Kotahi Mahuta,
Chairman of the Tainui Māori Trust Board

Introduction by Angela Ballara

AUCKLAND UNIVERSITY PRESS
DICTIONARY OF NEW ZEALAND BIOGRAPHY

Jointly published in 1996 by
Auckland University Press with Bridget Williams Books
Private Bag 92019, Auckland, New Zealand
and the Dictionary of New Zealand Biography
Department of Internal Affairs
P O Box 805, Wellington, New Zealand

Reprinted 1998

ISBN 1 86940 202 2

Cover design and typography by Mission Hall Design Group
Design and layout by Afineline
Typeset by Archetype, Wellington
Printed by GP Print Ltd, Wellington

The Dictionary of New Zealand Biography gratefully
acknowledges the assistance of the General Fund of the
New Zealand Lottery Grants Board.

Te Kīngitanga is produced with the support of
Te Arikinui Dame Te Ātairangikaahu, Sir Robert Mahuta
and the Tainui Māori Trust Board

Contents

Foreword

Teenaa koutou. This book brings together the lives of our tuupuna who created the Kiingitanga. Such a collection is really for our mokopuna and their descendants, for it is in their hands that the future of the movement lies.

We should recall the derivation of the word mokopuna. As one of our kaumaatua explained, it brings together two concepts.

A puna (spring) provided the only mirror our people knew. Moko was of course the identifying carved facial tattoo. So when a rangatira looked into the puna he saw his own reflection. This image of identity reflected becomes the word that we use for our children and their descendants.

We greet this book which will do so much to enable our mokopuna to see how the old people sought to create a new collective identity. The need was great, for new times required a new bonding of the iwi when contact with Paakehaa first occurred. Unity was not achieved without difficulty and dissent, and at many times seemed so fragile that the movement might not survive. In fact it has and what will become of it will be illuminated by understanding that background.

This is not a standard history of Kiingitanga for that is yet to be written. Rather, it is from these lives that the voices of the past are calling to us, for history is still in the making.

Pai Maarire.

R. T. Mahuta
Principal Negotiator
Waikato Raupatu Settlement

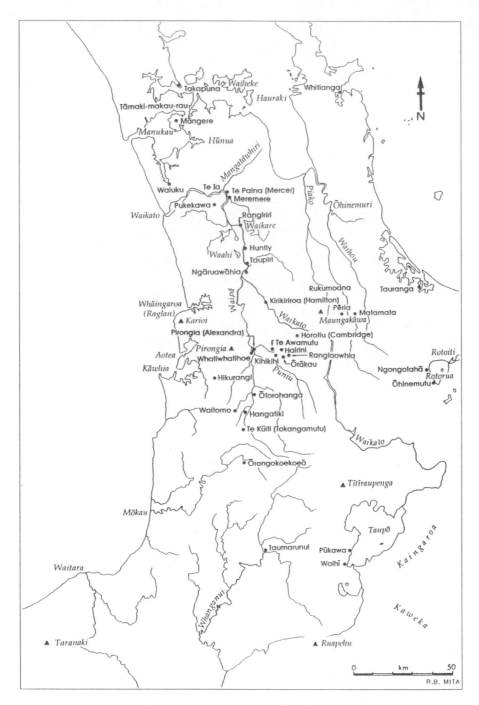

Sketch map of locations, central North Island.

Introduction

The King movement's first hundred years

'He rā e tō, he rā e puta mai anō.'

The emergence of the kingship

From its origins in the 1850s, the King movement was the first effort to create a Māori nation, a new polity with which to confront the onslaught of colonisation. The pan-Māori appeal of the movement is illustrated by Māori accounts of the selection of the first King.[1] Most agree that the King movement began at Ōtaki.

In 1852 Tāmihana Te Rauparaha, son of Te Rauparaha, the Ngāti Toa conquerer of the Kapiti coast, was presented to Queen Victoria in England. Impressed with her power, he wanted his father to support his ambition to become King of New Zealand. But Te Rauparaha reminded his son that his power was limited; Ngāti Toa had left Kāwhia because the Waikato peoples were too strong for them. It is said that Tāmihana's cousin, Mātene Te Whiwhi, had the ancestry of many possible candidates for kingship examined by the genealogical experts Te Hūkiki and Whīoi; they found Pōtatau Te Wherowhero of Ngāti Mahuta to be the most qualified.[2]

However, the kingship was first offered to Te Ānaua, and then to Tōpia Tūroa, but both the lower and upper Whanganui chiefs declined the burden. After canvassing Wairarapa without success the kingmakers passed on to Ahuriri in Hawke's Bay, where the important chiefs were such rivals that no one could be invited. They went on to the East Coast, where Te Kani-a-Takirau considered he was already a king. At Taupō, Iwikau Te Heuheu Tūkino turned down the offer; Te Muera Amohau of Te Arawa also refused. Some accounts mention other leaders. The King

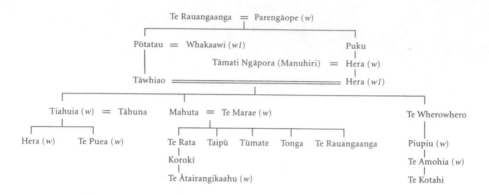

Some of the kāhui ariki.

movement newspaper, *Te Hōkioi*, later recorded that about this time a government interpreter ridiculed the idea that Māori should have a king: the Queen was a person of great possessions; a Māori king would be poor. This gave Te Heuheu the idea that Pōtatau should be chosen: his people were rich in resources, and he lived in the centre of the island surrounded by all the most powerful tribes. The kingmakers travelled to Waikato-taniwha-rau (Waikato of the hundred chiefs).[3]

When Wiremu Tāmihana Tarapīpipi Te Waharoa of Ngāti Hauā heard of their arrival he went to Mānuka (Manukau) where Pōtatau then resided, to support his election as King. Pōtatau refused, seeing no need for such a title for himself; for 15 generations in the direct male line his ancestors had been ariki and he could trace his whakapapa from every major founding canoe.[4] There were seven other meetings – at Haurua, Taupō, Maungatautari, Rangiaowhia, Paetai, Ihumātao and Ngāruawāhia – before Pōtatau eventually agreed.[5] One of the most important was at Haurua, near Ōtorohanga, hosted by Ngāti Maniapoto. The people there hailed Pōtatau as King, but he pointed to Tanirau of Ngāti Maniapoto as the proper candidate. Tanirau, however, saluted Pōtatau as King, who replied, 'the sun will set' – meaning that he was too old and would soon die. But Tanirau said, 'He rā e tō, he rā e puta mai anō' (the sun may set, but it soon rises again).[6] These words were crucial to Pōtatau's acceptance of the kingship, and determined its ongoing and hereditary nature.

Kaitotehe pā, home of Pōtatau Te Wherowhero, painted by George French Angas
in 1844. Taupiri Mountain is in the background.

At the last meetings before Pōtatau's election the title of King was debated: some wanted him to be called the Father of the Tribes, others Ariki Taungaroa (chief of chiefs), Toihau (supreme head), Rangatira (chief); other titles were proposed. But Te Moananui of Hawke's Bay argued that since there were many chiefs the title King should be used. The King should be unique; none must be of similar rank.[7] Reluctantly, Pōtatau accepted his destiny; he was crowned at Rangiaowhia, and again at Paetai or Rangiriri. Ngāruawāhia was the last crowning; there all the leading chiefs of the North Island came to lay at Pōtatau's feet their lands and service. Many mountains, the pou (boundary markers) of the Rohe Pōtae (the King movement territory), were named as the guardians of the territory under Pōtatau's dominion. They included Karioi, between Whāingaroa (Raglan) and Aotea; Taranaki (Mt Egmont); Kaiiwi, a hill in Ngā Rauru territory in Taranaki; Tararua, between Wairarapa and the Kapiti coast; Tītīokura, between Hawke's Bay and Taupō; Pūtauaki (Mt

Edgecumbe) in the Bay of Plenty; Ngongotahā, near the western side of
Rotorua; and Te Aroha, between the Ōhinemuri and Piako rivers.[8]

The assertion of self-rule

Contemporary European accounts of the King movement confirm widespread Māori support in the late 1850s for the creation of a Māori King.
The pressures of European colonisation – the rapid influx of land-hungry
Europeans, the methods they used to acquire land, and the effects of land
sales and the monetary economy on Māori social organisation –
intensified this support. The worst problems arose from new ways of
dealing with property in land. Before European settlement Māori land
tenure customs did not include land alienation by sale; there were few
chiefs with the mana or authority to 'tuku' or gift land, a transaction
which was not the same as outright alienation. The Crown had acquired a
pre-emptive or sole right of purchase of Māori lands through the Treaty of
Waitangi. Although this might have protected Māori custom and inter-
ests, it had the opposite result: the Crown became a vigorous and mono-
polistic purchaser, buying land in ways that caused divisions in Māori
society. At first open meetings had discussed land purchases, but from the
late 1840s land was often bought secretly by government officials or
without proper enquiry into its ownership, from Māori individuals or
groups who did not represent all the owners. Before colonisation these
sellers would not have had the right to gift land, let alone to alienate it.

   Although there had been disputes and wars with settlers and with the
government over land from the outset of settlement, by the 1850s most
Māori leaders were equally concerned about disputes between Māori.
Before and after the foundation of the British colony in 1840, Māori
identified themselves as members of local hapū (descent groups). Their
broader ties were to other hapū descended from a common ancestor,
sometimes including entire iwi (peoples or tribes). Still wider links were
based on traditions of descent from the crews of founding canoes. But
they did not regard themselves collectively as a single people, the Māori
nation. They were māori – indigenous to the country – as distinct from

tauiwi (alien). To control individuals, Māori communities had relied on the ties of kinship, deference to recognised chiefs, public meetings, consensus, and community pressure. After 1840, in the new and more complex society, the old ways were often inadequate. Many Māori leaders had attended missionary committees or magistrates' hearings to settle disputes with Europeans and had experienced other legal procedures; some thought them better fitted to the needs of the new situation.

By the early 1850s Māori leaders had often expressed their wish for a system of courts and policing, and some form of inter-tribal authority. These they would have to provide for themselves since the office of protector of aborigines had been abolished in 1846, and the young colony had many calls on the public purse; providing a court system or inter-tribal administration for Māori was a low priority. Before his departure in 1853, Governor George Grey had relied on a system of personal influence and persuasion, for the most part leaving Māori chiefs to resolve their own disputes, provided they did not resort to what had formerly been the ultimate sanction, warfare. The result was social disharmony and weakening of relationships. Faced with a threatened breakdown of communities, Māori leaders across the country sought new ways of controlling their lands and people.

Unable, on their own, to prevent the irresponsible sale of land by individuals, or clandestine sales by one group of lands claimed by another, Māori leaders banded together, separately in Taranaki and Waikato, to prevent the sale of any lands within their areas. In Taranaki, during 1853 and 1854, two rūnanga (assembly) houses were built in the Ngāti Ruanui district. The largest was Taiporohēnui ('the coast where the great wrong will end'), said to have been named by Mātene Te Whiwhi; the smaller was called Kumeamai. A huge meeting was held in Taiporohēnui in May 1854, attended by representatives of many Taranaki and Whanganui tribes, and a group from Ōtaki led by Tāmihana Te Rauparaha and Mātene Te Whiwhi. Its object was to unite the tribes from Kurukuru (near New Plymouth) to Kaiiwi (near Wanganui) in an agreement to hold all the land within those boundaries. Those who joined swore to maintain the tapu of the land on pain of death. The first attempt to break the tapu in August 1854 met with violent opposition; Rāwiri Waiaua and four others were killed.[9] The same month, officials reported that a group of Waikato chiefs had laid a tapu preventing the sale of any lands within designated boundaries. When Māori living at Manukau attempted to sell their claims on the lower Waikato river banks in September, a large armed party travelled down the river to set up boundary marks beyond which no sales were permitted, 25 miles from the Waikato Heads.[10]

From these first efforts at self-determination, the idea of the kingship rapidly gained ground. It became a focus of Māori efforts to transcend tribal rivalries and create a national organisation capable of maintaining Māori control over Māori destinies and of resisting the rapidly increasing settler authority, now expressed through the settlers' own parliament. The precise form of the King movement evolved gradually. For some time the idea of a Māori kingdom was complemented, and sometimes rivalled, by a growing interest in local Māori self-government through rūnanga or local councils. One suggestion was to set up an annual rūnanga of deputies from all the tribes.[11] When Iwikau Te Heuheu called his meeting at Pūkawa (near Taupō) in November 1856 at which this rūnanga system was introduced, the election of a king was also discussed, and the candidacy of Pōtatau Te Wherowhero was again mooted. The more turbulent spirits wanted to drive all Pākehā into the sea; this idea was expressed in a night meeting in a large house illuminated with many candles. As at Taiporohēnui, a chief walked around the house during the debate, quietly putting out the candles.[12] The lesson was understood; the light represented the ministers, teachers and all Pākehā who had demonstrated good will and whose skills were regarded as useful. Some of these were European runholders on leased land who chiefs expected would provide useful revenue if land sales were prevented and leasing encouraged.[13]

About February 1857 Wiremu Tāmihana became firmly committed to the King movement. He was a man of great natural talents, combining intellect and leadership. At crucial times in the development of the movement he was able to articulate clearly the choices which lay open to supporters of the Kīngitanga and to explain their benefits and dangers.[14] In 1857 he led a rūnanga in which the chiefs of Ngāti Hauā considered how they might achieve the rule of law. Tāmihana took their ideas to the government's Native Office in Auckland. For two days he asked for an interview to discuss the plan. But, while Europeans who visited the office were immediately attended to, he was rudely rebuffed and ignored. The Taupiri missionary B. Y. Ashwell recorded Tāmihana's response: 'Then I said to myself – We are treated like dogs – I will not go again. I then went to Māngere and I said to Pōtatau – go back to Waikato and let us consider some tikanga [rules] for ourselves'.[15]

Wiremu Tāmihana was only one among the many 'kingmakers', yet, partly because of his ability to provide the Kīngtanga with a clear, logical agenda, his advocacy was vital to its ultimate establishment. Like other chiefs he supported Pōtatau because of his past as a great warrior and, more recently, as the protector of the tribes of the Auckland isthmus.[16] His status as ariki, his kin connections with many iwi, and the wealth of Ngāti Mahuta were other considerations. A King could only carry out his role if his people and lands could sustain the burden of continuous hospitality on a grand scale. Tāmihana, a consummate politician, had one further reason for supporting Pōtatau: his good relations with successive governors, the respect they showed him and his protection of Pākehā Auckland from Māori threats. As early as 1841, Governor William Hobson had reported to London that Pōtatau was the most powerful chief in New Zealand.[17]

A meeting with the governor was held at Paetai in mid-April 1857; there it became clear that while the King party wanted Pōtatau to agree to be King, they also wanted friendly relations with the governor. Another party wanted to draw up their own laws, to be sanctioned by the governor, and administered by European magistrates and Māori assessors.[18] The demands for law expressed at this meeting led to the appointment of F. D. Fenton as resident magistrate for Waikato and Waipā and the introduction of an official rūnanga scheme. But this was too little and too late. Further meetings later in the same month culminated at Rangiriri, where Pōtatau agreed to be elected King. He was crowned and anointed at Ngāruawāhia in June 1858, Wiremu Tāmihana taking a prominent role in the ceremony.

Māori saw the Kīngitanga as a spiritual force 'carried' from marae to marae. Its physical manifestations – the King's flags, the pātaka (carved storehouses) and rūnanga houses, the mountains named as pou (supports) or rohe (boundaries) – were imbued with tapu and the mana of the kingdom. In handing over their lands to the King and placing them under his mana, his far-flung subjects hoped to keep the lands and their communities together by removing the temptation of ready money through selling. The lands placed under Pōtatau were to become the 'Crown lands' of the Māori kingdom.[19]

For their part, contemporary Europeans questioned the purpose of the kingship: was it a land league or was it merely a quest for law and order? Did it challenge British sovereignty and was it opposed to the spread of Pākehā settlement? But these Pākehā questions were irrelevant to Māori, for whom the Kīngitanga was a development *for* Māori, not *against* Europeans. Māori were at a loss to understand why Pākehā saw the movement as a threat to the Queen's sovereignty. As they saw it, the Pākehā governor was to rule over Europeans, and over any Māori living on lands that had gone to the Queen through purchase. The Māori King was to rule over his subjects and lands within the Rohe Pōtae. The Queen's power was a protective fence around the whole country, and over all was God.[20]

In its inception, the Kīngitanga was close to being a national organisation;[21] the kingship had been offered in turn to most of the ariki who were also reigning chiefs, paramount in their areas of the North Island. Chiefs from many districts placed their lands and, in a few cases, their people under the mana of the King. The Rohe Pōtae originally included Hauraki, Waikato–Maniapoto, Kāwhia, Taupō, Mōkau, parts of Taranaki, the upper Whanganui, the upper Rangitīkei and Tītīokura. Except in Waikato–Maniapoto, Kīngitanga supporters were often in a minority and worked within the divisions and factions born of local politics, but the movement had strong support in Tauranga, Hawke's Bay, Taranaki, lower Whanganui, Manawatū, and Wairarapa. The principal tribal groups that held out from the Kīngitanga were the Northland tribes, most of Te Arawa, most of Ngāti Porou and the other peoples of the East Coast, and most of the South Island. But there was strong interest and pockets of support even in those areas which rejected formal – or any – allegiance to the King.[22]

The crucible of war

The outbreak of war in Taranaki in 1860 made war in Waikato seem inevitable, at least to Europeans. Apart from a few lonely voices, Pākehā persisted in seeing the influence of the King movement behind Wī Kīngi Te Rangitāke's resistance to the taking of his Waitara lands. To them it was a nationalistic Māori threat to British sovereignty and settler expansion. They proclaimed that there was no choice but to force Māori into sub-jugation. Those Europeans, such as the missionaries Octavius Hadfield and T. S. Grace, who argued that the King movement could be tolerated as a form of local self-government, were persistently discredited as idealists, or even as traitors. The actions of Kīngitanga supporters were regularly misinterpreted. Some Ngāti Maniapoto went to fight for Wī Kīngi, and when he returned their help by putting his lands under the Māori King, the rabid enemies of the King movement felt justified in their hostility. In fact, most of the King supporters of lower Waikato, including Pōtatau himself, opposed involvement in the Taranaki war.[23] This was well known, but ignored. When Wiremu Tāmihana attempted to make peace in Taranaki in 1861, this effort was misinterpreted as recruitment for the King's land league. That he was successful in sending many belligerents away from the battlefield was not taken into account.[24]

As war in Waikato drew near, the early, fragile unity of the King move-ment was threatened by division. It became clear that old patterns of hapū, chiefly and individual independence had not disappeared. The Kings – Pōtatau and, after June 1860, his son Matutaera (later known as Tāwhiao) – and the chiefs supporting the King were not in control of all their followers. Wiremu Tāmihana led a group opposed to war; in 1861 he advised Europeans who visited him not to worry about the term King; his people were ready to accept magistrates and courts, and had never rejected the Queen's overall authority. Tāwhiao's advisers and immediate

URQUHART COLLECTION, ALEXANDER TURNBULL LIBRARY F4643½

Kakaramea (Razorback Hill) on the road constructed by the military in 1862 betweeen Drury and Pōkeno.

followers in Waikato formed another party, also moderate and committed to the peace policies of Pōtatau. A more extreme group among Ngāti Maniapoto was responsible for most of the violent incidents and was ready to fight if challenged.[25]

The challenges came: the appointment of John Gorst as resident magistrate was seen as an attempt to supplant the King's rūnanga; Gorst's newspaper, *Te Pīhoihoi Mokemoke*, a rival to *Te Hōkioi*, ridiculed the King movement. A number of aggressive actions raised the political temperature and signalled the determination of Governors Gore Browne and Grey and the colonial government to put down the Kīngitanga. These included the plan to build a court house which could double as police barracks at Te Kohekohe, the construction of government roads to Mangatāwhiri and Whāingaroa, the erection of a redoubt at Te Ia, and the plan to place bullet-proof steamers on the Waikato River.

The government made no real attempt to negotiate, merely issuing proclamations in June 1861 and July 1863 demanding submission.[26] At Taupiri in January 1863, in a pronouncement that reverberated throughout the movement, Grey threatened to dig around the Kīngitanga until it fell. Tāmihana was provoked into writing a reply saying that just as different nations in Europe had sovereigns from among their own people, Māori should also be able to choose one of their own. He cited the biblical command from Deuteronomy 17:15: 'one from among thy brethren shalt thou set king over thee: thou mayest not set a stranger over thee, which is not thy brother.'[27] Though Tāmihana did not reject the Queen's authority, his reply was taken as proof that sovereignty was at the root of the confidently expected Waikato 'rebellion'. Rumours flew – about Māori attacks on Auckland, Pākehā attacks on the King's territory, and the stockpiling of arms. Settlers and missionaries withdrew from Waikato, there were violent incidents, and the government's occupation of Tataraimaka in Taranaki was resisted in May. War in Waikato drew closer. A proclamation dated 11 July 1863 declared that Māori who did not take the oath of allegiance would lose their lands; government forces crossed the Mangatāwhiri River (the Kīngitanga boundary) and fought the first battle before its text had been seen in Waikato.[28]

When Waikato was invaded, the various divisions within the Kīngitanga came together to defend the kingdom. Unity was born of adversity, but this was the only benefit to the King movement. The Kīngitanga forces enjoyed some victories but suffered more disastrous defeats. The attack by imperial troops on Rangiaowhia, the undefended village where non-combatants had been sent,[29] left a legacy of bitterness and suspicion. The war came to an end in Waikato and Tauranga in 1864, but continued in Taranaki with the rise of the Hauhau movement. In Hauraki, Wiremu Tāmihana, always aware of the futility of fighting, made a separate peace in May 1865.[30] The Kīngitanga forces of Waikato–Maniapoto withdrew to the south of the forward British posts of Te Awamutu and Kihikihi, and entrenched themselves at Haurua and Hangatiki.[31] Behind this line and the Puniu River the King movement remained undefeated and isolated.

For nearly two decades after 1865[32] the aukati or King's boundary could not be safely crossed by unescorted Europeans or kūpapa (neutral

Māori).[33] The land within the aukati became known to Europeans as the King Country. It was a state within a state, governed by the King's rather than the Queen's writ. Colonial forces remained on the defensive towards it. Māori committing crimes outside the aukati and 'rebels' such as Te Kooti could take refuge within it, remaining safe from pursuit. The King and his supporters prevented most traffic across the border in either direction, even trade and missionary activity. In this isolation Tāwhiao gradually developed the principles of the modern Kīngitanga.

Retreat and rebuilding

The kingdom had shrunk through land confiscations authorised under the New Zealand Settlements Act 1863: a huge area was confiscated late in 1864 and gazetted in 1865. It was defined by rivers, passes, mountain tops and coastal stretches, with straight lines between the named points. From the Hauraki Gulf across to the Waikato Heads, the confiscated area stretched south to Whāingaroa, eastwards across to the Waitetuna River, south via Pirongia to the Puniu River and its junction with the Waipā (near Te Awamutu), eastwards across to Ōrākau (near Kihikihi), to Pukekura (near Cambridge), north-east to Maungākawa, in a straight line to Pukemoremore and back to Hauraki.[34] This land has been estimated at 1.2 million acres; subsequently just over 314,000 acres were returned by Crown grant to neutrals and 'returned rebels'. The government took most of the lower Waikato district, including some of the lands of neutral tribes and a third of the lands of Ngāti Hauā. Ngāti Maniapoto, whose people included the most belligerent, had little land taken.[35] This lopsided choice convinced King supporters that the whole war had been deliberately engineered to acquire the fertile lands closest to Auckland for settlement.[36] Confiscation ensured that suspicion of government remained a binding force among Kīngitanga supporters. The land losses of the Waikato tribes, when compared to the almost untouched lands of Ngāti Maniapoto, were to shape the internal politics of the King movement for a generation.

Though from 1864 to 1872 rumours abounded suggesting Kīngitanga involvement with the warlike Hauhau wing of the Pai Mārire movement,

Tokanganui-a-noho, the house built for Tāwhiao at Te Kūiti in 1878.

the main thrust of the Kīngitanga from that time was towards peace. Settlers feared a general uprising in 1866, but Tāwhiao and his principal advisers were not actively involved. It was often assumed that the Hauhau were 'Kingites'; for officials the two terms were almost synonymous. When Tāwhiao and many other leaders adopted the peaceful Pai Mārire faith, this reinforced the illusion of a single Kingite–Hauhau enemy. At this time, Tāwhiao had in fact little influence over the other Kīngitanga leaders. His principal adviser was his 'uncle' (cousin in a senior generation), Tāmati Ngāpora. By 1867 Tāwhiao and Ngāpora had both declared that 'the sword was sheathed';[37] neither deviated from this pacifist stance. During the military campaigns of Tītokowaru (on the west coast) and Te Kooti (on the east coast and inland), both beginning in 1868, speculation was rife in Pākehā newspapers and official correspondence that these leaders and their followers would unite with the Kingites in a general uprising. But Tāwhiao did not support Tītokowaru,[38] and refused to acknowledge Te Kooti's presence in the King Country until he too 'sheathed his sword'. Te Kooti later acknowledged that Tāwhiao had taught him the message of peace.[39]

The Kīngitanga supporters took refuge with Ngāti Maniapoto at Tokangamutu, known later as Te Kūiti, where they developed a large settlement with extensive cultivations. Here Tāwhiao periodically announced his isolationist policy. While declaring that the fighting should stop, he also forbade a number of activities within his dominion: land selling, land surveying, the operations of the Native Land Court and Māori assessors, levying of rates, building roads and the telegraph, and gold-prospecting. These policies were maintained throughout his reign.

By 1873 Tāwhiao's passive resistance policies had been accepted by most of his followers, and he took a more controlling role in the movement. He rejected war but at the same time refused to make peace with the government until the confiscated lands were returned. This gained him growing support. On a visit to Kāwhia and Aotea that year he took the worst troublemakers with him to keep them quiet. He replaced his father's friends and councillors, who he said had committed murders, with his own 'lambs', whose work would be providing for his people. Landless Waikato people who promoted war in revenge for the confiscations were outnumbered from this time by those committed to peace.[40]

These developments were accompanied by religious changes. For a while the King movement supported the Tekau-mā-rua, 12 men appointed by Tāwhiao as his representatives within the spiritual and political movement led by Te Whiti and Tohu of Parihaka.[41] In 1875 and 1876 the Tariao faith was adopted after it had been introduced by Tāwhiao. It revived the Pai Mārire prayers and adopted new forms of ritual. The Tariao were ministers of the new faith; Tāwhiao communicated with them in a series of pānuitanga (announcements), which exhorted them to obey a new list of rules, again banning roads, telegraphs, surveys, rates and land selling, and also some older Māori customs: these were taua muru (punishing raids), exhumation of bodies, the use of tohunga (priests) for cursing enemies, and the imposition of tapu. Tāwhiao was regarded as the head Tariao; his sister, Tīria, was the leader of the female Tariao ministers or ngehe. The sacred character of the kingship was reinforced in this faith: in his exhortations to his followers, Tāwhiao associated the name of God with his own, and increasingly used prophetic and profound language to characterise the kingship.[42]

From the 1870s some King supporters began to withdraw their allegiance. Some hapū of Ngāti Tūwharetoa and Ngāti Raukawa living on the east bank of the Waikato River were seeking work on public roads from 1870 on, although those on the west bank, nearer to Te Kūiti, remained staunch King supporters.[43] Tribes outside the Rohe Pōtae, in spite of having placed their lands under the King's mana, allowed the Native Land Court to sit and recommenced selling land. The King's stricter supporters, while rejecting land sales and the court, dreaded further war and wanted to ease relations between the King and the government. A meeting was arranged between Tāwhiao and Donald McLean, now native minister, at Waitomo in 1875. Waikato King tribes were offered reserves of land on the west bank of the Waikato River in return for taking the oath of allegiance, but Tāwhiao would accept nothing less than the return of all the confiscated lands. Though it had little result, the meeting was seen by the King's followers as opening the way for further contact with the government.[44]

Relations between the Waikato tribes and their Maniapoto hosts had been poor ever since their arrival. Ngāti Maniapoto feared that Waikato would commit some act that would lead to confiscation of Maniapoto lands; they also feared Waikato would claim the land on which they were living. The King supporters were in fact anxious to leave, as relations between the two groups worsened.[45] A new centre was established at Hikurangi, on a ridge between Kāwhia and the Waipā River, 18 miles from Alexandra (Pirongia), and the bulk of Tāwhiao's Waikato supporters moved there in 1877.[46]

By this time, the tradition of the 'Maehe' had become established: annual hui in March at which the King's subjects renewed their allegiance and their committment to oppose land selling. Sir George Grey, now premier, attended the Maehe of 1878. The King's supporters regarded his visit as another step on the way to normal relations with the colonial

ALEXANDER TURNBULL LIBRARY 25749½

Governor Jervois meets Kāwhia chiefs in 1884 while Tāwhiao is away in England.

government without retreating from Kīngitanga aims. At the Hikurangi settlement huge cultivations were developed out of virgin forest, an eight-mile road was cut through to Kāwhia Harbour, and Tāwhiao permitted a European from Alexandra to set up a water mill to thresh the settlement's wheat.[47] Development continued until 1881. That year Tāwhiao met Major William Mair in Alexandra, a meeting which symbolised lasting peace,[48] and a new Kīngitanga centre was set up at Whatiwhatihoe, near Alexandra on the opposite side of the Waipā.[49] Each move brought the Waikato supporters of the King movement closer to trading contacts with settlers and, while remaining within the aukati, back towards their own lands. Europeans who had feared a military alliance between the King, Te Kooti and Parihaka welcomed these signs of goodwill.[50]

The King movement, however, was continuing to lose strength through the defection of those who chose to forget their covenant with Tāwhiao. Large sections of Ngāti Maniapoto, Tūwharetoa and others were determined to put the Rohe Pōtae and other blocks through the Native Land

Court and to allow the main trunk railway to pass through their territory. But as the movement was progressively stripped of the less committed, there remained a steel core of determination centred around Tāwhiao himself.

In 1882 the native minister, John Bryce, attempted to bribe Tāwhiao with a pension, a position as Legislative Councillor, the return of 20,000 acres of confiscated lands and a furnished house. He was expected to take the oath of allegiance and to open the King Country to settlement through roads, the railway and the Native Land Court. Tāwhiao refused.[51] Encouraged by the efforts to court him, he continued to bargain for independent authority and the complete return of the confiscated lands. In 1884 the King movement raised money for its leaders to visit Britain and present a petition alleging breaches of the Treaty of Waitangi, asking for home rule and requesting an independent investigation into the causes of the Waikato war. The delegation met Lord Derby at the Colonial Office, but was told the imperial government had no power to coerce the New Zealand Parliament.[52] The utter lack of benefit from this effort and the continuing defection of former supporters undermined the isolation of the Kīngitanga and forced the movement to turn to other solutions.

New initiatives, new divisions

From 1886 'King committees' operated at Whatiwhatihoe, Kāwhia, Aotea, Thames and Ōhinemuri. In effect they provided local government within Kīngitanga territory and operated in opposition to the government-sponsored committees set up under the Native Committees Act 1883. They issued summonses, heard cases, opposed surveys and blocked government works wherever possible.[53] At the same time, the establishment of a separate Māori parliament and government was set in train. In 1886 a petition was sent to the native minister for a Māori legislative council but it did not reach the Native Affairs Committee.[54] The only response was a further offer to Tāwhiao of a seat in the colonial Legislative Council. Undeterred, the Kīngitanga made plans for its own parliament, the Kauhanganui, which was set up at Maungākawa near Cambridge about

Whatiwhatihoe in November 1884.

1889–90. Each year after its founding, the King was enthroned on 2 May. One of the purposes of the parliament was that Tāwhiao could communicate with his people through the tribally appointed delegates.[55]

Meanwhile, in the early 1880s, conditions at Whatiwhatihoe had moved towards a crisis. The land was not fertile enough to support a permanent population of any size. Partly to relieve supply problems there, and partly to increase support in other regions, Tāwhiao went on progresses to Kīngitanga marae throughout the North Island, always accompanied by hundreds of supporters. These visits were later institutionalised as the Poukai: annual ceremonial visits to enable the King to meet the people and to gather revenue. But even long absences at other marae could not solve the problem. The Land Court in 1886 began to work in the Rohe Pōtae, so that the Kīngitanga centre could not be moved south. Kāwhia or Aotea were options, but there Tāwhiao's followers would have been isolated from the Waikato tribes. The centre could not be moved north without moving on to confiscated land. In 1888 Tāwhiao was forced to choose between land awarded to his followers in the Compensation Court

Tāwhiao's house at Whatiwhatihoe.

or the dispersion of his people. He chose to accept the land and a new settlement was developed at Pukekawa, close to Mercer.[56] He moved again in 1893 to Pārāwera, south-east of Kihikihi and south-west of Maunga-tautari.[57] These moves gave the kūpapa tribes of the lower Waikato an opportunity to rejoin the Kīngitanga and so heal former divisions.[58] They also took the Kīngitanga back into areas close to Ngāti Hauā, most of whom had been physically separated from the movement since 1863.[59]

In the same period, relations with Ngāti Maniapoto were improving. Rewi Maniapoto, estranged from Tāwhiao since 1877, had returned to the Kīngitanga fold in 1884.[60] By 1890 his kinsman Wahanui Huatare was one of the King's chief advisers, and in December 1891 Tāwhiao was able to make a ceremonial visit to Te Kūiti and Ōtorohanga.[61] By the time of Tāwhiao's death and the accession of his son, Mahuta, in 1894, other Kīngitanga issues had emerged as more important than the remaining tensions between Waikato and Ngāti Maniapoto. One of these was the kingdom's continued integrity. Since his reign began, Tāwhiao had maintained his independence in the face of numerous government attempts to subvert him. In 1892, however, he accepted a government pension. Tāwhiao justified his action as a test of the government's sincerity in promising that he could retain the title of King and control local Māori affairs. Other Waikato leaders were outraged, and Tāwhiao was forced to abandon the experiment.[62]

This episode showed that earlier divisions continued. Indeed, the King movement in the nineteenth century had rarely been united except in extreme adversity. Strong leaders led their followers towards common but differently expressed goals. This pattern persisted through Mahuta's reign (1894–1912), Te Rata's reign (1912–33), and in the reign of his son, Korokī. These divisions were not absolute; the aims of the leaders continued to intersect and to weave, like a river delta, taking different courses but heading in the same direction.

One branch of the delta was followed by Mahuta. The desperate economic plight of his people induced him to test the government's goodwill as Tāwhiao had done in 1892. From 1898 Prime Minister Richard Seddon had pressed the King to accept a seat on the Legislative Council and in the cabinet. In 1903 Mahuta accepted the positions. No benefits were forthcoming, and the move was seen by many in the movement and outside it as an abandonment of the kingdom's independence.[63]

Mahuta's other schemes had no better outcome. Land blocks he had recovered through the Native Land Court were sold and money was invested in his name by Hēnare Kaihau. Mismanagement led to the loss of at least £50,000 of Kīngitanga funds.[64] Mahuta then attempted to re-establish Taupiri and Ngāruawāhia as a township for his people and the centre of the kingdom, again counting on government help. Again he was sorely disillusioned, although his land purchases at Ngāruawāhia would later provide a place for the Kīngitanga's reconstruction. In the face of these disasters Mahuta changed his plans. Few of his people had received Pākehā secondary education, while other tribes now had tertiary graduates to guide them into the twentieth century. Although prevented by previous political ties from openly committing himself, in 1911 Mahuta secretly approved the efforts of his son, Te Rata, and his niece, Te Puea Hērangi, to recruit an educated candidate, Dr Māui Pōmare, for the

Premier Richard Seddon (seated, centre) meets Mahuta at Waahi in 1898.
King Mahuta is seated on Seddon's left; James Carroll stands to Seddon's right.

parliamentary seat of Western Māori. Many Kīngitanga supporters hoped that this was the way to secure the return of the confiscated lands.[65]

Mahuta's attempts to work with the government were fiercely rejected by the branch of the movement led by Tupu Taingākawa Te Waharoa, the second kingmaker. Taingākawa had earlier been a disciple of Tāwhiao; he now sought to take on his mantle as the guardian of the kingdom's independence. Together with others who shared his ideas, he worked through institutions set up under the Kauhanganui to achieve mana motuhake (autonomous power) for the Kingdom of Aotearoa. Following its constitution set up in 1894, the Kingdom sought to provide itself with revenue, civil and land courts, and police. It did so under the direction of a cabinet of ministers (like earlier Kīngitanga councils called the Tekau-mā-rua), which continued to oppose the Native Land Court, the rating of

Māori lands and the jurisdiction of Pākehā legal institutions in Kīngi-tanga territory. The movement's newspaper, *Te Paki o Matariki*, published at Maungākawa in Taingākawa's Ngāti Hauā territory, publicised the activities of this government.[66]

Taingākawa and his supporters, and many who disapproved of Mahuta's actions, sought to aggrandise Taingākawa's role of Tumuaki (leader) of the Kauhanganui; he sought to assume part of the King's role himself. In 1907 a Kotahitanga (federation or union) of Aotearoa and Te Waipounamu was set up at Waahi.[67] It recognised the hereditary nature of Taingākawa's position as Tumuaki, accepted a rāhui (reserve) on lands under his protection, declared his seal the only legitimation of its acts, and established a covenant for his followers to sign. A 1910 hui at Waha-roa confirmed this Kotahitanga, which took as its charter the second clause of the Treaty of Waitangi. Early in his reign Te Rata was strongly influenced by Taingākawa. In 1914 he went with him to England to peti-tion the Crown to revoke the confiscations as a breach of the Treaty of Waitangi. Although the petitioners were received by King George V and Queen Mary, as in 1884 the journey was without any tangible result.[68]

Drawing together again

During the First World War the Kīngitanga once more drew together to face an external threat, this time the issue of conscription. Throughout the war Kīngitanga leaders, now joined by Te Rata's cousin Te Puea Hērangi, maintained a united front of opposition to conscription. Two of the royal brothers, Tonga and Te Rauangaanga, were arrested and dragged off like common criminals to do their military service. The Kīngitanga saw no reason to fight for the government; there had been no redress on the matter of confiscation. Further, the government's studied refusal to acknowledge the special status of the kāhui ariki (royal family) caused great offence.[69]

Living at Waahi, near Huntly, King Te Rata, his brothers and other leaders, in common with other branches of the King movement, never ceased to demand an acknowledgement that Waikato had not rebelled but had rather defended themselves against attack. The land confiscations were therefore unjust and the land or its equivalent should be returned. Resisting the efforts of Taingākawa to involve them in his Kauhanganui and Kotahitanga activities, and of Te Puea to bring them back to Ngāruawāhia and Taupiri, they held on to the established rituals at Waahi. Meanwhile, Taingākawa and his supporters had re-established a new Kauhanganui at Rukumoana in Ngāti Hauā territory. Gradually Te Rata and other kāhui ariki became offended at his efforts at supremacy.

When Taingākawa approached the spiritual and political leader, T. W. Rātana, for support in 1920,[70] Te Rata's misgivings were reinforced. Taingākawa persuaded the Rātana movement to adopt the Treaty of Waitangi as its charter and with Rātana took a further petition to Britain in 1924. Though these activities may have contributed to the setting up of the Sim Commission in 1927, which decided in favour of the Kīngitanga position that the confiscations were unjustified, many Kīngitanga leaders saw the Rātana movement as a threat to the King's mana. Rātana himself was sometimes accused of trying make himself King of the Māori;[71] most Kīngitanga leaders felt that if there was to be a national Māori King movement, Te Rata's kingdom had the prior claim.

But the major development of the 1920s was the rising influence of Te Puea. Following the plan conceived by Mahuta, she sought to re-establish Ngāruawāhia as the centre of the Kīngitanga. In 1921 she moved there with her followers and spent the next 20 years establishing a community which grew from the most Spartan beginnings to the assured success symbolised by the houses Māhinārangi, Tūrongo and Kimikimi. In the 1920s she raised funds for the needs of the community by means of a travelling concert party. She was able to enlist the help of the native minister, Āpirana Ngata, and the funds he administered to develop Waikato lands for the support of the kingdom and of the impoverished Waikato people.

The Waikato tribes did not universally support Te Puea until Te Rata and his brothers accepted the consolidation and development plans she had drawn up with Ngata. Together they set about restoring what Te Puea described as their 'ruined kingdom',[72] through economic development

The house Māhinārangi at Ngāruawāhia, opened in 1929.

and compensation for the confiscations. Te Rata's brother, Tūmate Mahuta, led the negotiating team seeking redress, but in 1936 his efforts suffered from the interference of another kingmaker, Tarapīpipi, the son of Tupu Taingākawa. The kāhui ariki were seriously angered, and from this time the kingmaker's role was limited to ceremonial functions.[73] The negotiations were interrupted by the Second World War, but a settlement reached in 1946 set up the Tainui Māori Trust Board to administer the compensation funds accepted as the best compromise then available. The board received £6,000 per annum initially, with a later reduction to £5,000.

While the efforts of the leaders to take their people out of the economic decline caused by confiscation identified the kingdom more strongly with Waikato–Tainui, the Kīngitanga also continued to seek national recognition for Te Rata's successor, Korokī, as Māori King. Te Puea's nationwide reputation helped to give the movement a supra-tribal character.

Tūrongo, the house built for King Korokī by Te Puea,
with Māhinārangi in the background.

The media, which had discovered her in 1927, bestowed on her the title of 'princess' – and this presupposed a kingdom. Her cultural revivals of waiata and dance, canoe building (for the 1940 centennial), marae development schemes throughout Waikato, and assistance to the Red Cross and other patriotic activities during the Second World War, all contributed to the image of a paramount Māori institution.

By 1948 hotel owners in the 'dry' King Country were pressing for the granting of liquor licences. Kīngitanga leaders tried to prevent the change. They considered that in 1885 the premier of that time, Robert Stout, had agreed to a sacred pact: in return for sanction to build the main trunk railway the Rohe Pōtae was to remain dry. An inquiry found that a verbal pact had been made but that such an agreement could not bind subsequent governments. King Korokī led a delegation to Wellington to gain recognition of the Kīngitanga standpoint. He failed to alter the government's decision, but the published photos of 600 Māori following their

King Korokī with Lady Bledisloe, wife of the governor general.

The Kauhanganui house (later Tūrangawaewae House), Ngāruawāhia.

King into Parliament left a deep impression on the public.[74] The Kīngi-tanga was alive, strong, and would live on.

In their search for government recognition of the special status of the King, the Kīngitanga leaders enjoyed many successes. But the question remained: did honours and favours for its leaders, Te Puea and Korokī, mean government recognition of the King's mana, or were these merely a new round of political bribes?[75] Lord Bledisloe, governor general in 1934, had told the young Korokī, 'I need you to be a figurehead for your people',[76] but such a position was devoid of authority. To successive governments, the Kīngitanga was still a movement that had begun as subversive and continued as separatist. Its opposition to conscription in the First World War had not been forgotten, and in the Second World War Prime Minister Peter Fraser demanded an assurance of loyalty. Contemporary constitutional theory declared sovereignty to be one and indivisible; how then could a small country accommodate an institution which claimed to be an autonomous kingdom?

But these, like the objections to the Kīngitanga in the 1850s, were Pākehā problems. For Māori, the Kīngitanga was an abiding reality, whatever its divisions and difficulties. As Robert Mahuta wrote in 1978: 'so long as it has meaning and relevance for its adherents then so long will it continue.'[77]

Almost a century and a half since its first beginnings, the Kīngitanga or Māori King movement is a continuing force in New Zealand society. A unique institution, it continues to preserve and transmit the spiritual and political standpoints (tūrangawaewae) of the past while providing practical leadership to many present-day Māori and in the national political arena. Its strongest support lies in and around Ngāruawāhia and Taupiri. From this base the Kīngitanga gives leadership to many of the Tainui tribes of the central North Island and retains binding links with areas which were part of the original Rohe Pōtae.

Kīngitanga efforts to secure redress from the government have at last produced significant results. On 3 November 1995 Queen Elizabeth II signed into law the Waikato Tainui Raupatu Claims Settlement Bill in the presence of the Māori Queen, Dame Te Ātairangikaahu, the principal Tainui negotiator, Robert Te Kotahi Mahuta, and other Tainui elders. The new act, agreed to in December 1994, formalised a settlement between the government and Tainui. Crown reparation included some land, funds to the value of $170 million, and a formal apology for the confiscations and the devastation caused by British forces in the 1860s warfare.

From the founding of the Kīngitanga, each generation of leaders had sought redress for its legitimate grievances. Strength for the struggle had been drawn from the people's declaration of identity:

Ko Taupiri te maunga   *(Taupiri is the mountain*
Ko Waikato te awa   *Waikato is the river*
Ko Te Wherowhero te tangata.   *Te Wherowhero is the man.)*

Angela Ballara

References

1. Māori accounts include: *Te Hōkioi o Nui-Tīreni e Rere Atunā*, 15 June 1862, p.3; Eric Ramsden, Letters received 1930–1942 from Princess Te Puea Hērangi and Alex McKay, Micro MS 534, Alexander Turnbull Library (account of the founding of the Kīngitanga in letter of 14 June 1933); Leslie G. Kelly, *Tainui*, Wellington, 1949, p.439ff.; Pei Te Hurinui [Pei Jones], *King Pōtatau*, Wellington, 1960, p.206–209; Pei Te Hurinui Jones, 'Māori Kings', in *The Māori people in the nineteen-sixties*, ed. Eric Schwimmer, Auckland, 1969, p.132–134; John Te H. Grace, *Tūwharetoa*, Wellington, 1959, p.442–457.

2. Ramsden, Letter from Te Puea, 14 June 1933; Jones, 'Māori Kings', p.133.

3. *Te Hōkioi*, 15 June 1862, p.2.

4. Kelly, p.479 (Genealogical Table 84).

5. *Te Hōkioi*, 15 June 1862, p.3.

6. Ramsden, Letter from Te Puea, 14 June 1933.

7. Jones, 'Māori Kings', p.133; *Te Hōkioi*, 2 June 1862, p.3.

8. *Te Paki o Matariki*, 25 June 1893, p.3.

9. *Appendices to the Journals of the House of Representatives (AJHR)*, 1868, A–1, p.19, No 12, Report from R. Parris, civil commissioner, Taranaki (re 1853–54); Richard Taylor, Journals, entries for 8 May 1854, 22 Dec. 1857, 23 Dec. 1858, Typescript, Auckland Institute & Museum Library.

10. *AJHR*, 1862, C–1, p.105–106, No 3, J.G. Johnson to chief commissioner, Donald McLean, 6 Oct. 1854; B. Y. Ashwell, Letters to the Church Missionary Society, Taupiri, 21 Sept. 1854, Typescript, Auckland Institute & Museum Library.

11. *AJHR*, 1862, C–1, p.323, No 20, District commissioner, G. S. Cooper, to chief commisioner, Donald McLean, 29 Nov. 1856.

12. Ashwell, Letter of 20 Aug. 1857.

13. *AJHR*, 1862, C–1, p.323.

14. As he did at the Pēria meeting in 1862. Accounts of this meeting are in *Te Hōkioi*, 10 Nov. 1862; J. E. Gorst, *The Māori King*, London, 1864, p.318–320.

15. Ashwell, Letter of 1 May 1861.

16. F. D. Fenton, *Important judgements delivered in the Compensation Court and Native Land Court, 1866–79*, Auckland, 1879, p.75 (Ōrākei judgement).

17. *AJHR*, 1861, C–1, p.167, No 5, Governor Hobson to secretary of state, 15 Dec. 1841.

18. Ashwell, Letters of 20 Aug. 1857, 30 May 1861.

19. *Te Hōkioi*, 15 June 1862, p.4 (letters from chiefs and tribes dated 1859).

20. Ashwell, Letter of 1 May 1861.

21. *Te Hōkioi*, 15 June 1862, p.1–4; *AJHR*, 1883, G–1, p.4, No 2, G. T. Wilkinson to under-secretary, Native Department, 11 June 1883.

22. *Te Hōkioi*, 15 June 1862, p.1–4; *Te Paki o Matariki*, 25 July 1893, p.5.

23. Ashwell, Letter of 1 May 1861; Gorst, p.159; *AJHR*, 1874, G–2B, p.5, R. S. Bush to native minister, 14 Oct. 1873; *AJHR*, 1876, G–1, p.8, No 11, Bush to native minister, 9 Feb. 1876.

24. Ashwell, Letter of 30 May 1861; William Fox, *The war in New Zealand*, London, 1866, p.36.

25. Ashwell, Letters of 20 Aug. 1857, 30 May, 11 July 1861, 1 May 1862; John Morgan, Letters and journals, Report of Oct. 1860, Typescript, Auckland Institute & Museum Library.

26. Alan Ward, *A show of justice*, Auckland, 1973, reprinted with corrections 1995, p.129.

27. Gorst, p.176; *AJHR*, 1868, A–1, p.76, No 49, Governor Sir G. F. Bowen to the Duke of Buckingham, 30 June 1868.
28. Gorst, p.378, 380; Ward, p.159.
29. James Cowan, *The New Zealand wars*, Vol.1, *1845–64*, Wellington, 1922, p.352.
30. Ashwell, Letter of 6 June 1865.
31. Cowan, p.408–409.
32. J. H. Kerry-Nicholls, *The King Country*, London, 1884, p.7, 15, 25.
33. *AJHR*, 1867, A–1A, p.10, Encl. 6 in No 6, Civil commissioner, Tauranga, to native minister, 25 Oct. 1866; 1868, A–1, p.74, No 49, Sir G. F. Bowen to the Duke of Buckingham, 30 June 1868; 1868, A–4, p.11, No 6, Report from H. T. Clarke, civil commissioner, Tauranga, 7 March 1868.
34. *New Zealand Gazette*, 5 Jan. 1865, p.1–2.
35. *AJHR*, 1866, A–1, p.95, No 29, Governor Sir George Grey to Right Hon. Edward Cardwell, MP, 3 May 1866.
36. *AJHR*, 1866, A–1, p.95; 1868, A–4, p.4–5, No 3, Report from W. N. Searancke, resident magistrate, Hamilton, 9 March 1868.
37. *AJHR*, 1868, A–4, p.5.
38. *AJHR*, 1868, A–4, p.21; A–8, p.16–17, No 18, Hōri Kīngi to Mete Kīngi Paetahi, 22 July 1868; p.47, No 92, R. Parris to Hon. J. C. Richmond, 12 Aug. 1868; James Belich, *The New Zealand wars*, Auckland, 1986, p.256.
39. Judith Binney, 'Myth and explanation in the Ringatū tradition', *Journal of the Polynesian Society* 93, No 4 (Dec. 1984), p.366; Binney, *Redemption songs*, Auckland, 1995, p.272.
40. *AJHR*, 1873, G–1, p.21–22, No 23, W. G. Mair to native minister, 12 June 1873; p.24, No 25, R. S. Bush, resident magistrate, Raglan, to native minister, 16 June 1873; G–1B, p.7, No 5, H. T. Clarke to native minister, 30 Jan. 1873; 1874, G–2B, p.4–5, No 7, Bush to native minister, 14 Oct. 1873; p.6, Bush to native minister, 22 Nov. 1873; p.9–10, Encl. in No 9, Speech extracts at Poihakene [*sic*], Raglan, 28 Nov. 1873.
41. *AJHR*, 1873, G–1, p.22; 1874, G–2B, p.4; 1878, G–1, p.8, No 10, R. S. Bush to native minister, 25 May 1878.
42. 'He ōhākī nō te Kīngitanga o Pōtatau Te Wherowhero, o Tāwhiao', 1860–1878, Pānuitanga from Hikurangi, 29 [?month], Sept., 10 Dec. 1875, 16 Aug. 1876, MS, University of Auckland Library; *AJHR*, 1876, G–1, p.2, No 4, R. S. Bush to native minister, 12 Oct. 1875; p.2–3, No 5, 15 Oct. 1875; p.5–7, No 9, Bush to native minister, 8 Jan. 1876; 1880, G–4A, p.1, W. G. Mair to under-secretary, Native Department, 29 May 1880.
43. *AJHR*, 1871, F–6, p.3, Encl. in No 1, S. Locke to J. D. Ormond, 29 Oct. 1870; p.5–7, Encl. in No 2, Locke to Ormond, 2 Feb. 1871; No 3, Donald McLean to Ormond, 13 Feb. 1871; Encl. in No 4, Locke to Ormond, 13 May 1871; 1873, G–1B, p.6; 1874, G–2, p.9; 1875, G–1, p.1–2, No 1, R. S. Bush to native minister, 1 April 1875.
44. *AJHR*, 1875, G–1, p.1–2, No 1, R. S. Bush to native minister, 1 April 1875; p.8, No 7, Bush to native minister, 5 May 1875; p.14, No 9, R. W. Woon, resident magistrate, to under-secretary, 21 May 1875; G–1A, p.2; M. P. K. Sorrenson, 'Māori and Pākehā', in *The Oxford history of New Zealand*, 2nd ed., ed. Geoffrey W. Rice, Auckland, 1992, p.160.
45. *AJHR*, 1875, G–1, p.9; 1877, G–1, p.5–6, No 7, W. G. Mair to under-secretary, Native Department, 25 May 1877; p.8, No 9, R. S. Bush to under-secretary, Native Department, 8 May 1877; 1878, G–1, p.8–9.
46. *AJHR*, 1878, G–3, p.1–71, Reports of meetings between the . . . Premier [Sir George

Grey] . . . and natives; p.15, Extract from the *New Zealander*, 7 May 1878.

47. *AJHR*, 1878, G–1A, p.2, No 2, R. S. Bush to native minister, 17 June 1878; G–3, p.4, 15–40; *Auckland Weekly News*, 22 Feb., 11 April 1879, 3 Jan. 1880; *AJHR,* 1880, G–4A, p.1, No 1, W. G. Mair to under-secretary, Native Department, 29 May 1880; 1881, G–8, p.4, No 5, Mair to under-secretary, Native Department, 27 May 1881; *Waikato Times*, 10, 12 & 17 May 1881.

48. *Te Paki o Matariki*, 6 Oct. 1892, p.3, col.1.

49. *Auckland Weekly News*, 3 Sept. 1881; *Waikato Times*, 27 April, 8 July 1882.

50. *New Zealand Herald*, 3 Oct. 1882, lead article; Jones, 'Māori Kings', p.137.

51. *Waikato Times*, 4 & 11 Nov. 1882.

52. *AJHR*, 1884, G–1, p.11–12, G. T. Wilkinson to under-secretary, Native Department, 14 May 1884; p.17–18, No 9, James Booth, resident magistrate, to under-secretary, Native Department, 1 May 1884; *Waikato Times*, 28 Feb., 26 & 31 July 1884, 13 Oct. 1885; *Te Paki o Matariki*, 6 Oct. 1892, p.4, col.2–p.5.

53. *Te Paki o Matariki*, 6 Oct. 1892, p.5; *AJHR*, 1886, G–1, p.4, No 5, G. T. Wilkinson to under-secretary, Native Department, 25 May 1886.

54. *AJHR*, 1886, G–1, p.8; *Te Paki o Matariki*, 6 Oct. 1892, p.7, col.1; *Waikato Times*, 13 & 20 April, 13 May, 10 July 1886.

55. *Te Paki o Matariki*, 8 May 1893, p.3, col.1.; 6 Oct. 1893.

56. *AJHR*, 1888, G–5, p.3–5, No 4, G. T. Wilkinson to under-secretary, Native Department, 2 June 1888; *Auckland Weekly News*, [cutting not fully identified], 1886; *Waikato Times*, 14 April, 6 Oct. 1888, 24 April 1890; *AJHR*, 1889, G–3, p.3, No 4, G. T. Wilkinson, native agent, Alexandra, to under-secretary, Native Department, 20 June 1889; 1890, G–2, p.2, 5, No 4, Wilkinson, Ōtorohanga, to under-secretary, Native Department, 19 June 1890; 1891, G–5, p.5, No 3, Wilkinson, annual report to under-secretary, Native Department, 10 June 1891.

57. R. T. Mahuta, 'Tāwhiao, Tūkaroto Matutaera Pōtatau Te Wherowhero', in *The Dictionary of New Zealand Biography, Volume Two, 1870–1900*, Wellington, 1993, p.509–511.

58. Michael King, *Te Puea*, Auckland, 1977, p.51.

59. Jones, 'Māori Kings', p.140.

60. *AJHR*, 1884, G–1, p.11–12.

61. *AJHR*, 1892, G–3, p.4, G. T. Wilkinson to under-secretary, Native Department, Ōtorohanga, 28 June 1892.

62. *Te Paki o Matariki*, 9 Aug. 1892; *AJHR*, 1892, G–3, p.6.

63. Seddon family papers, MS Papers 1619, folder 30, Alexander Turnbull Library; *Te Puke ki Hikurangi*, 30 June 1899, p.3, col.1; 15 Aug. 1899, p.5, col.2–3; *Te Pīpīwharauroa*, Jan. 1903, p.10.

64. Jones, 'Māori Kings', p.144.

65. ibid.

66. *Te Paki o Matariki*, 1892–1914, passim.

67. *Te huihuinga ki Waharoa, Aperira 7, 1910*, Hamilton, 1910.

68. *Te Kōpara*, April 1914, p.5, 8; MA Series 1, 1914/2202, National Archives.

69. Māori Under Military Service Act: Correspondence, AD Series 1, Sub-series 66/11, National Archives; P. S. O'Connor, 'The recruitment of Māori soldiers, 1914–18', *Political Science*, 19, No 2 (1967), p.61ff.

70. *Te Whetū Mārama*, 29 March 1924, p.5; J. M. Henderson, *Rātana*, Wellington, 1963, p.27

71. *Te Toa Takitini*, 1 Aug. 1930, p.2126; *Te Whetū Mārama*, 13 Feb. 1932.
72. Ramsden, Letter from Te Puea, 14 June 1933.
73. Ramsden, Letter from Alex McKay, 26 Aug. 1936; King, *Te Puea*, p.259.
74. *AJHR*, 1885, G–1, p.8, Notes of a meeting between the Hon. Mr Ballance and Wanganui Māori at Ranana, 7 Jan. 1885; p.18, 20, Meeting at Kihikihi, 4 Feb. 1885; *New Zealand Herald*, 13 July 1923, p.4, 9; 13 & 17 Nov., 1 Dec. 1948; *Auckland Star*, 31 March 1949; King, *Te Puea*, p.256.
75. King, p.193.
76. Ramsden, Letter from Te Puea, 8 April 1934.
77. Robert Mahuta, 'The Māori King Movement today', in *Tihe mauri ora*, ed. Michael King, Wellington, 1978, p.40.

Select Bibliography

Appendices to the Journals of the House of Representatives (New Zealand). 1861–1892

Ashwell, B. Y. Letters to the Church Missionary Society. Typescript. Auckland Institute & Museum Library

Binney, J. *Redemption songs*. Auckland, 1995

Cowan, J. *The New Zealand wars*. Vol.1, *1845–64*. Wellington, 1922

Gorst, J. E. *The Māori King*. London, 1864

Grace, J. Te H. *Tūwharetoa*. Wellington, 1959

'He ōhākī nō te Kīngitanga o Pōtatau Te Wherowhero, o Tāwhiao'. MS. University of Auckland Library

Henderson, J. M. *Rātana*. Wellington, 1963

Jones, P. Te H. 'Māori Kings'. In *The Māori people in the nineteen-sixties*. Ed. E. Schwimmer. Auckland, 1968

Kelly, L. G. *Tainui*. Wellington, 1949

Kerry-Nicholls, J. H. *The King Country*. London, 1884

King, M. *Te Puea*. Auckland, 1977

Mahuta, R. 'The Māori King movement today'. In *Tihe mauri ora*. Ed. M. King. [Wellington], 1978

Ramsden, E. Letters received 1930–1942 from Princess Te Puea Hērangi and Alex McKay. Micro MS 534. Alexander Turnbull Library

Sorrenson, M. P. K. 'Māori and Pākehā'. In *The Oxford history of New Zealand*. 2nd ed. Ed. G. W. Rice. Auckland, 1992

Taylor, R. Journals. Typescript. Auckland Institute & Museum Library

Te Hōkioi

Te Hurinui, P. [P. Jones]. *King Pōtatau*. [Wellington, 1960]

Te Paki o Matariki

Te Whetū Mārama o te Kotahitanga

Ward, A. *A show of justice*. Auckland, 1973 (reprinted with corrections, 1995)

Part One

Pōtatau Te Wherowhero

Wiremu Tāmihana Tarapīpipi Te Waharoa

Te Wherowhero. Painting by George French Angas.

Pōtatau Te Wherowhero
?–1860

Tainui and Ngāti Mahuta leader, first Māori King

Te Wherowhero was born in Waikato towards the end of the eighteenth century. He was the eldest son of a Waikato warrior chief, Te Rauangaanga, and Parengāope of Ngāti Koura. He belonged to the senior chiefly line of Ngāti Mahuta, and was descended from the captains of the Tainui and Te Arawa canoes. Te Wherowhero had four wives, Whakaawi, Raharaha, Waiata and Ngāwaero. His children were Matutaera (later known as Tāwhiao), Te Paea Tīaho and Tīria (also known as Te Otaota or Mākareta).

Te Wherowhero grew up in the period of peace that followed the great victory of Waikato over Ngāti Toa in the battle called Hingakaka, at Te Mangeo, near Lake Ngāroto. He was taught traditional lore by his father and later learned sacred knowledge at Te Papa-o-Rotu, the Waikato whare wānanga at Whatawhata. He also trained as a warrior, and when his relative Te Uira was killed by Ngāti Toa, he took part in warfare against them. He is said to have instigated the killing of Marore, a wife of Te Rauparaha, while she was visiting relatives in Waikato about 1820. After revenge killings by Ngāti Toa, an army of Waikato and Ngāti Maniapoto warriors invaded Kāwhia in 1820, and defeated Ngāti Toa at Te Kakara, near Lake Taharoa, and Waikawau, south of Tīrua Point. Te Rauparaha was then besieged at Te Arawī, near Kāwhia Harbour, and after negotiations it was agreed that Ngāti Toa should cede their lands to Waikato and depart for the south. They were allowed to leave and at first went to Te Kaweka, in northern Taranaki.

Te Wherowhero then led a large army in pursuit. He was also going south to the aid of Peehi Tūkorehu, a Ngāti Maniapoto leader, whose war party was besieged at Pukerangiora, on the Waitara River, by Taranaki tribes. In late 1821 or early 1822 the Waikato army suffered a military disaster at Motunui; against Te Wherowhero's orders it charged a feigned retreat of Ngāti Toa and its allies. Te Wherowhero refused to join the retreat that followed and remained by the body of a slain Waikato chief, where Ngāti Toa and their Ngāti Mutunga allies found him. A man of Ngāti Mutunga would have shot him, but was stopped by Te Rauparaha. Te Wherowhero then fought a number of chiefs in single combat, armed only with a digging implement. Waikato forces returned to join him and both armies retired. It is said that at night Te Wherowhero approached the Ngāti Toa camp and asked Te Rauparaha for his advice. Te Rauparaha directed him south to Pukerangiora, to avoid a Taranaki army to the north. Te Rauparaha's assistance to Te Wherowhero was probably due to their common descent from the people of the Tainui canoe. Te Whero-whero went to Pukerangiora and raised the siege of the Waikato warriors there before returning to Waikato. He returned in time to lead Waikato against an invasion by the musket-armed Ngā Puhi of Hongi Hika.

Hongi Hika was seeking revenge for the deaths of several relatives at the hands of Waikato allies in Tāmaki and Hauraki. He led 3,000 warriors to the Waitematā Harbour; they dragged their canoes to the Manukau Harbour, and went from there to the Waikato River by way of the Awaroa Stream. Waikato delayed the invaders by felling trees into the stream. They concentrated their defence at Mātakitaki pā, where 10,000 people gathered under Te Wherowhero's command in May 1822. When Ngā Puhi attacked, a panic seized the defenders, many of whom had not ex-perienced musket warfare before. There was a rush to escape the pā and many people were trampled to death. Te Wherowhero led a defensive fight, at one point single-handedly.

After the fall of the pā, Ngā Puhi split into small groups to hunt for fugitives. At Ōrāhiri, near Ōtorohanga, a large group of Ngāti Mahuta women were captured. Te Wherowhero had retreated towards the Rangitoto Range and was cautiously moving back down the Waipā River when he met an old woman who had escaped. He sent her back to tell the women that they would be rescued as soon as the morning star rose. At this hour the enemy warriors were asleep, except for one who was drinking from the river. He was quietly drowned and the rest of that group of Ngā Puhi were killed. Waikato settled further south for several years, for fear of further Ngā Puhi attacks. Te Wherowhero lived at Ōrongokoekoeā on the upper Mōkau River. His wife, Whakaawi, gave birth there to their son Matutaera. When peace was made with Ngā Puhi in 1823, Waikato gradually returned to their homes. The peace was cemented by the marriage of Te Wherowhero's close relative, Kati, to Matire Toha of Ngā Puhi. Their daughter was called Te Paea.

Hongi Hika came to Waikato again in 1825 in pursuit of Ngāti Whātua fugitives, but he did not attack Waikato. However, in 1826 Pōmare I led Ngā Puhi to invade Waikato while Te Wherowhero was at Taupō. Te Wherowhero wished to go and meet Pōmare, but was dissuaded by Te Kanawa, who feared treachery. Pōmare and his army went up the Waipā River and were defeated, and Pōmare killed, at Te Rore. In 1827 Waikato forces went to Tāmaki to assist Ngāti Pāoa against a Ngā Puhi attack, and Te Wherowhero then led a canoe fleet to attack Ngā Puhi at Whāngārei. Waikato won a battle at Ōparakau, after which peace was arranged and Waikato returned home. On this expedition Te Wherowhero wore a cloak of red kākā feathers, from whose colour his name is sometimes said to be derived.

Warfare with Ngāti Hauā about 1830 forced Ngāti Maru north towards Hauraki, and by this time Ngāti Raukawa had migrated south to Manawatū. This left Waikato free to seek revenge for their defeat at Motunui by Taranaki tribes. In 1831 Te Wherowhero led an expedition into Taranaki and attacked Te Āti Awa. They took refuge at Pukerangiora, but did not have time to gather food for a long siege. After three months the pā fell when its inhabitants attempted to escape in daylight. They were massacred, and many were eaten. It is said that Te Wherowhero killed 150 prisoners with his mere, Whakarewa. His army, however, failed to take the pā at Ngāmotu, near present day New Plymouth, and returned home.

Ngā Puhi raided Waikato again in 1832 but were driven off by 3,000 Waikato warriors, most of them armed with muskets. The firearms had been obtained from the trader J. R. Kent, who had settled at Kāwhia and married Tīria, the daughter of Te Wherowhero. The name Pōtatau may have been taken by Te Wherowhero at the time of this marriage.

Te Wherowhero continued his attacks on Taranaki tribes between 1833 and 1836. He had been provoked by a raid on the Mōkau River by Te Āti Awa. He besieged several pā, with varying degrees of success. Mikotahi pā, on an island near Ngāmotu, was supplied by sea and proved impregnable. At Te Namu, near Ōpunake, Ngāti Ruanui drove off five assaults by Waikato, but Te Ruaki pā, near Hāwera, was forced to surrender after a siege of three months. After an unsuccessful attack on Waimate pā, at the mouth of the Kāpuni Stream in 1836, Te Wherowhero made peace with the Taranaki people and withdrew, saying that he would not return.

Missionaries arrived in Waikato in the mid 1830s. Their growing influence was demonstrated by the release in 1840 of slaves taken during the Taranaki wars. Although he attended church services, Te Wherowhero was never baptised. In March 1840 Captain W. C. Symonds brought a copy of the Treaty of Waitangi to Manukau, where Te Wherowhero was living at Te Awhitū. He refused to sign the treaty but was kindly disposed towards the European government. In May 1844 he provided a huge banquet for a great intertribal gathering at Remuera. His influence at the meeting impressed on Governor Robert FitzRoy the fact that Auckland's security depended on Waikato friendship. In the 1840s Te Wherowhero's cottage at Pukekawa, in the Auckland Domain, was the scene of much discussion of issues arising from the signing of the Treaty of Waitangi. He was one of the chiefs who sold land to the government in the Manukau area. However, he protested to Queen Victoria over the 1846 instruction from Earl Grey, secretary of state for the colonies, that all land not actually occupied or cultivated by Māori was to be regarded as Crown property, in contravention of the guarantees of the Treaty of Waitangi. In 1848 Te Wherowhero was one of those who accompanied Te Rauparaha's return to his people at Ōtaki, on his release from government custody. At Governor George Grey's request Te Wherowhero and some of his followers moved to Māngere and in 1849 he signed an agreement to provide military protection for the city of Auckland.

A movement arose in the 1850s to establish a Māori king to protect

The tomb of Pōtatau Te Wherowhero.

Māori land from alienation and to make laws to end internal strife. Mātene Te Whiwhi travelled throughout New Zealand seeking a chief of high standing who was willing to be king. Iwikau Te Heuheu Tūkino III, of Ngāti Tūwharetoa, suggested that Te Wherowhero should be approached, and his choice was supported by Wiremu Tāmihana, of Ngāti Hauā. Te Wherowhero was reluctant to take on the role of peacemaker while the death of one of his relatives, Rangiānewa, at the hands of Ngāti Hauā in 1825, was unavenged. Peace was made, however, and after lengthy negotiations Te Wherowhero accepted the kingship, and was installed at Ngāruawāhia in 1858. In his speech of acceptance he stressed the spirit of unity symbolised by the kingship, likening his position to the 'eye of the needle through which the white, black and red threads must pass.' He enjoined his people to 'hold fast to love, to the law, and to faith in God.'

Te Wherowhero never regarded the kingship as being in opposition to the sovereignty of Queen Victoria, and wanted to work co-operatively with the government. Some of his associates, however, sought to prevent or hinder government activities in areas which supported the King. Te Wherowhero opposed their levying of port dues on ships at Kāwhia Harbour, and threatened to leave Waikato and return to Māngere if tribute continued to be demanded from government mail canoes using the Waipā River.

Te Wherowhero had been much consulted by Governors George Grey and Thomas Gore Browne on matters concerning Māori. However, after his acceptance of the kingship he was increasingly estranged from the governor's confidence. As land disputes increased in number and severity Te Wherowhero was in many cases forced into a position of opposition to government policy.

Pōtatau Te Wherowhero died at Ngāruawāhia on 25 June 1860. Many tribes gathered to pay their last tributes to him. He was succeeded as King by his son Tāwhiao.   *Steven Oliver*

Kelly, L. G. *Tainui*. Wellington, 1949
Te Hurinui, P. [P. Jones]. *King Pōtatau*. [Wellington, 1960]

Wiremu Tāmihana Tarapīpipi Te Waharoa
?–1866

Ngāti Hauā leader, teacher, diplomat

Tarapīpipi was the second son of Te Waharoa of Ngāti Hauā. His mother was Rangi Te Wiwini. He was born in the early nineteenth century, possibly about 1805, at Tamahere, on the Horotiu plains. As a young man in the 1820s he participated in several war expeditions in the Taranaki and Waikato districts. In 1825, in support of Ngāti Korokī kin, he led a retaliatory attack on Ngāti Hinetū, a sub-tribe of Ngāti Apakura, at a pā called Kaipaka, near Te Awamutu. In the battle Rangiānewa, younger sister of Te Kahurangi, grandmother of the Waikato leader Te Wherowhero, was killed. Reprisals were averted when Te Waharoa allowed Ngāti Apakura to settle on lands at Rangiaowhia which had been occupied by Ngāti Korokī. In the mid 1830s Tarapīpipi also participated in the fighting between Ngāti Hauā and Te Arawa, instigated by the killing of Te Hunga, a relation of Te Waharoa, by Haerehuka of Ngāti Whakaue in December 1835. In the fighting at Ōhinemutu in August 1836 Tarapīpipi interceded on behalf of two CMS mission workers, and led them to a place of safety when the mission premises were destroyed by Ngāti Whakaue.

Tarapīpipi came under the influence of Christian teachings when the Reverend A. N. Brown established a CMS station near Matamata pā in April 1835. Within six months Tarapīpipi had learned to read and write in Māori, and was writing letters on behalf of his father. The fighting in 1836 led to the abandonment of the Matamata mission, but in January 1838 Brown took over the Tauranga mission station, including Ngāti Hauā within his parish. Early in 1838 the missionary printer W. R. Wade visited

Matamata and described the son of Te Waharoa as 'a fine, clever, active young man named Tarapīpipi, one of the most forward in knowledge and most desirous to know. In the absence of Missionaries he used to take the lead in all school matters.' During 1838 Brown also noted Tarapīpipi's eagerness to discuss spiritual matters, and encouraged him in the idea of setting up a separate Christian settlement.

Te Waharoa died in September 1838 and Tarapīpipi found himself with a new leadership role among Ngāti Hauā. Te Ārahi was the eldest son of Te Waharoa, but it was Tarapīpipi who inherited his father's mana. He resisted pressure from the tribe to carry on Ngāti Hauā campaigns against Te Arawa. Brown considered that he possessed 'too much natural decision of character to be moved from his purpose by the anger of his country-men'. On 21 October 1838 at Maungamana, near Tauranga, Tarapīpipi was given an opportunity to exercise his powers of diplomacy, at a meeting of Tauranga and Ngāti Hauā people to discuss relations with Te Arawa. After a haka and a number of speeches were made urging war, Tarapīpipi, according to Brown, 'rose with his Testament in his hand and in a bold yet pleasing manner "witnessed a good confession" before his countrymen whom with holy courage he reproved, rebuked, exhorted.' Although matters were not resolved at this meeting and sporadic skirmishes did occur, Tarapīpipi's leadership and his efforts to abide by Christian ideals prevented a major battle.

On 23 June 1839 Tarapīpipi was one of the first converts to be baptised by Brown at Tauranga. He was given the name Wiremu Tāmihana (William Thompson), and embarked on a life of teaching and preaching in the Tauranga and Matamata districts. Edward Shortland, who visited Waikato in 1842, commented that Tarapīpipi was 'the most influential young chief of the tribe', having inherited the mana of his father and displaying the highly esteemed qualities of bravery and eloquence. Shortland also considered that Tarapīpipi had not abandoned all traditional beliefs, 'But he believes the Christ to be a more powerful Atua, and of a better nature; and therefore he no longer dreads the Atua Māori.' Tarapīpipi put into practice the Christian teachings he had embraced within a traditional Māori framework, and guided his people to do

NICHOLL ALBUM VII, ALEXANDER TURNBULL LIBRARY 46644½

Wiremu Tāmihana Tarapīpipi Te Waharoa.

likewise. The influence of missionaries was important, but qualities of intellect, and leadership, courage, eloquence and diplomacy, were of far greater significance in the life of Wiremu Tāmihana.

During 1838 construction began on a new pā, the Christian village of Te Tāpiri, not far from Matamata pā, north of present day Waharoa. By March 1839 about 300 people were living there and a chapel and school had been built. Tāmihana's rules for the settlement followed the precepts of the Ten Commandments.

In late December 1839 a fire destroyed the chapel, several houses and much of the fencing at Te Tāpiri. The community set to work constructing a new and much larger chapel, about 80 feet by 40 feet, and 20 or 30 feet high. The interior was decorated with tukutuku panels between wall posts made of smooth slabs of tōtara. In 1842 William Colenso considered it 'the largest native built house in New Zealand', capable of holding up to 1,000 people.

About the time of the establishment of Te Tapiri, Tāmihana had taken a wife, Ita, daughter of Pohepohe of Matamata. Late in 1839 she was in the mission at Tauranga receiving medical attention, but in May 1840 she died, at Te Tāpiri. Tāmihana later married Pare Te Kanawa (also called Wikitōria), another daughter of Pohepohe. They had at least two sons, Hōtene Tāmihana and Tupu Taingākawa (known in his youth as Tana), and two daughters, Hārete and Te Raumako (Te Reo).

During the 1840s Tāmihana was occupied mainly with tribal and community affairs. He taught in a school at Te Tāpiri, established farming among Ngāti Hauā communities, and traded surplus produce to Pākehā settlers in Auckland. On the diplomatic front he played an important role in resolving an incident and restoring stolen property after a large tribal gathering in Auckland in 1844, and in 1845 peacemaking feasts were organised with Te Arawa. Tāmihana also tried to cope with the effects of new diseases among his people and wrote to Bishop G. A. Selwyn in 1844 seeking a doctor to help stem the death rate among Ngāti Hauā.

In 1846 Tāmihana began construction of another Christian pā, at Pēria, although Te Tāpiri remained occupied through the 1840s. The pā was named after the biblical town of Berea (Acts 17:10). Tāmihana spent much of his time there during the 1850s. It was a model Christian community set on rolling hills south of Matamata pā. There were separate clusters of houses for each kin group, surrounded by fields of wheat, maize, potatoes and kūmara, and orchards, mainly of peach trees. There were large raised storehouses for food, and numerous pits for storing potatoes and kūmara. On one hilltop there was a large church, and a burial ground on another. There was also a post office, a flour mill, a schoolhouse with separate boarding houses for up to 100 boys and girls, and a large meeting house in a central position. Visitors to the school commented on the high standards of reading, writing and arithmetic achieved by students.

The establishment of a code of laws and effective administration of the laws were high priorities for Tāmihana. The rūnanga at Pēria provided local government and also dispensed justice, after discussion in the meeting house. While other Waikato and Ngāti Maniapoto hapū also held their own rūnanga, John Gorst, the Waikato civil commissioner, was particularly impressed with the rule of law among Ngāti Hauā, which he attributed to 'the character and personal influence of Wiremu Tāmihana and the chiefs by whom he is ... surrounded and supported. I never heard a complaint of injustice from the Europeans resident amongst his tribe.'

During the late 1850s Tāmihana became involved in the establishment of a Māori king. For this he was given the title 'Kingmaker' by Pākehā. A number of incidents, including a rebuff when he sought government support for his system of government for Ngāti Hauā, culminated in tribal meetings to consider resistance to further land sales and Pākehā encroachment, the potential disintegration of Māori society, and the need for political solidarity among Waikato, Ngāti Maniapoto and adjacent tribes. At an important meeting held at Pūkawa, Lake Taupō, in 1856, Iwikau Te Heuheu Tūkino III of Ngāti Tūwharetoa supported Pōtatau Te Wherowhero of Ngāti Mahuta as king. Te Wherowhero was reluctant to take the position. Tāmihana had already decided that Te Wherowhero was the appropriate person. On 12 February 1857 he wrote a letter to the chiefs of Waikato expressing the support of Ngāti Hauā, and suggesting a meeting of all Waikato and Ngāti Maniapoto tribes to ratify this. In May 1857, at a meeting at Paetai, near Rangiriri, there was considerable debate on the merits of a Māori king and the question of support for the governor and Queen Victoria. Tāmihana spoke strongly to express his concern for the establishment and maintenance of law and order within the tribes. He hoped that a Māori kingship would provide effective order and laws, unlike the Pākehā government, which allowed Māori to kill each other and only involved itself when Pākehā were killed.

Te Wherowhero was still reluctant to accept the kingship. Tāmihana's involvement in the death of Rangiānewa in 1825 was an obstacle, but this was removed when Te Raumako, a daughter of Tāmihana, was offered to Ngāti Apakura at Rangiaowhia. Peaceful relations between the tribes were restored. After further discussion at another meeting at Ihumātao, on the Manukau Harbour, a large gathering at Ngāruawāhia in June 1858 agreed to the installation of Pōtatau Te Wherowhero as the first Māori King. Tāmihana provided a statement of laws, based on the laws of God. The King would exercise power over people and lands, over chiefs and councils of all the tribes; the tribes would continue to live on their own lands, and the King would protect them from aggression. The ceremonial installation of the King was held at Rangiaowhia shortly after. A meeting at Ngāruawāhia on 2 May 1859 confirmed Te Wherowhero as holding the mana of kingship, in an alliance with Queen Victoria, with God over both. Tāmihana placed a Bible over Te Wherowhero's head, establishing part of the ritual which is still carried out by his successor for the successors of Te Wherowhero.

Tāmihana became deeply involved in maintaining tribal relationships and a system of Māori government within the King movement, against a background increasingly suspicious of Pākehā motives. In June 1860 Pōtatau Te Wherowhero died and was succeeded by his son, Matutaera, who later took the name Tāwhiao. Tāmihana was instrumental in setting up a Māori language newspaper, *Te Hōkioi e Rere Atu Nā*, for the King movement. The government responded with *Te Pīhoihoi Mokemoke*, published by John Gorst at Te Awamutu. Tāmihana maintained a precarious alliance among the chiefs, some of whom wanted to fight, others to co-operate with the Pākehā governor. When war broke out in Taranaki in 1860, Tāmihana assumed the role of negotiator and mediator between Māori and Pākehā. He travelled to Taranaki in March 1861 and arranged a truce. He refused to meet Governor Thomas Gore Browne in Auckland, fearing the same fate as Te Rauparaha, who had been taken from his people and exiled to Auckland from 1846 to 1848. On the government side there was growing suspicion of the role of Tāmihana and his power in the King movement, and fears of armed uprising. Tāmihana tried to calm the rising tensions.

On 21 May 1861 Browne issued a declaration accusing Waikato of violating the Treaty of Waitangi, and requiring Māori submission to the Queen's sovereignty. Tāmihana wrote a lengthy response, indicating, with reference to Scripture and Māori metaphor, that the King movement was an organisation to control Māori people, and was not in conflict with the

Queen's sovereignty. He then outlined the Māori perspective on events in Taranaki and expressed concern that the governor seemed intent on conflict. There were more meetings at Ngāruawāhia to discuss the situation. Tāmihana wrote more letters to the governor, reiterating that the Māori were not seeking war, and questioning the construction of roads and redoubts between Auckland and northern Waikato. Several CMS missionaries joined the debate, urging Tāmihana to withdraw from the King movement. Tāmihana agreed to meet the governor, but was dissuaded by other Māori leaders.

In September 1861 George Grey returned for another term as governor of New Zealand, and the pressure on the King movement was maintained. Tāmihana spent as much time as he could at Pēria, keeping his community together, trying to prevent the illicit sale of liquor by Pākehā traders, and keeping up his correspondence with tribal leaders and the government. He was not enthusiastic about Grey's proposals for native government, insisting that the rūnanga already established provided an appropriate system. Grey's proposals were discussed at several meetings, and again Tāmihana mediated, as concern increased over military activity north of the Mangatāwhiri River, the northern boundary of the King's territory during 1862.

In October 1862 a meeting at Pēria brought together Waikato, Hauraki and Ngāti Maniapoto leaders, as well as representatives of Tauranga and East Coast tribes. The principal issues discussed were opposition to the construction of roads into Waikato from Auckland and Raglan, a fair system for adjudication on land, control of Pākehā traders, and the failure of the governor to settle the dispute over Waitara.

War broke out again in Taranaki in May 1863. In spite of the efforts of Tāmihana to keep the peace, Ngāti Maniapoto, led by Rewi Maniapoto, favoured war against the Pākehā. There was now an open rift between Ngāti Hauā and Ngāti Maniapoto. Tāmihana still sought negotiations with the government, but, as Gorst recorded, government people 'did not like Tāmihana. Few Europeans knew him personally, and it was the fashion to believe him insincere.' In 1862 William Fox had expressed his distrust of Tāmihana's motives, and this attitude persisted in government circles through the 1860s. In July 1863, in a memorandum to Grey, the premier, Alfred Domett, wrote, 'It is now beyond all question that the Native Tribes of Waikato the most powerful in New Zealand are resolved to attempt to drive out or destroy the Europeans of the Northern Island, and to establish a Native kingdom under a Native king.'

A proclamation, issued by Grey on 11 July 1863, required submission to Queen Victoria. On 12 July, before it could reach the King and Waikato tribes, British imperial troops, under Lieutenant General Duncan Cameron, crossed the Mangatāwhiri River, and invaded the lands of the King and his people. Tāmihana wrote a number of letters to North Island Māori leaders, informing them of events in Waikato. He also wrote to A. N. Brown at Tauranga, warning him of the approach of war. Copies of these letters were passed to government people, who construed them as confirmation of their distrust of Tāmihana.

After the battle at Rangiriri in November 1863 Tāmihana again sought to negotiate peace, sending his greenstone mere to Cameron as a token of his good faith. Neither Grey nor government ministers were prepared to negotiate, or to release prisoners taken at Rangiriri and held in Auckland. The conquest of Waikato proceeded. The attack in February 1864 on Rangiaowhia, a village where women, children and old people had been sent, caused particular anguish to Tāmihana. The only fighting in which Tāmihana was personally involved was the action at Hairini which followed the attack on Rangiaowhia: 'then for the first time my hand struck, my anger being great about my dead, murdered, and burnt with fire, at Rangiaohia'. Tāmihana returned to the pā called Te Tiki-o-te-ihinga-rangi, on Maungatautari. In April he and his people quietly abandoned the pā overnight and retreated to Pēria. Tāmihana wrote again to Grey and to other Māori leaders, seeking peace negotiations. The Waikato campaign shifted to Tauranga, with battles at Gate Pā in April and at Te Ranga in June 1864. Tāmihana offered to mediate, but was ignored.

On 17 December 1864 a proclamation was issued by Grey, confiscating a large area of Waikato and Ngāti Hauā lands. Military settlements were established in the Waikato, Waipā and Tauranga districts, and the tribes

The first kingmaker, Wiremu Tāmihana.

retreated beyond the boundary of confiscated land. There was some further correspondence between Tāmihana and government officials, and a letter from Grey in January 1865 suggested a meeting, which was not immediately arranged. In April Tāmihana submitted a petition to Parliament outlining a Māori view of the causes of the war, and seeking redress for the confiscations. There was no immediate response, but in May Tāmihana followed up earlier moves to meet Brigadier General G. J. Carey.

On 27 May 1865 Tāmihana laid down his taiaha before Carey at Tamahere, and agreed that the Queen's laws would also be the laws for the Māori King. Among Pākehā this act was described as a surrender. Tāmihana described it in a letter to Grey as 'te maungārongo' (the covenant of peace), indicating that arms had been laid down on both sides. Scepticism and distrust were again expressed by Pākehā leaders. Stung by accusations of insincerity, the pain of the misinterpretation of his 1863 letter to Archdeacon Brown, and the label of rebel, Tāmihana sent another petition to Parliament on 18 July 1865. He sought an impartial court of inquiry to investigate events in Waikato. The government response was to send a resident magistrate to talk to him. The interview was inconclusive and no inquiry ensued. Tāmihana wrote more letters to Grey and met him in Hamilton early in May 1866. He was persuaded to go to Wellington, ostensibly to give evidence before a parliamentary committee. On 24 July he presented another petition to Parliament, seeking a return of confiscated lands and a proper inquiry into the causes of the war. The petition was referred to the superintendent of Auckland province and no further action was taken.

In spite of illness, already apparent on his Wellington visit, Tāmihana maintained his involvement in tribal affairs. He attended sittings of the newly established Native Land Court, and mediated in disputes with surveyors in the Tauranga district, where land had also been confiscated. By October his health was deteriorating. He died at Tūranga-o-moana, near Pēria, on 27 December 1866. The missionary Richard Taylor wrote: 'There is something very sad in the death of this patriotic chief; a man of clear, straight-forward views; sad that a man, who possessed such an influence for good, should thus have been ignored by the Government, when, by his aid, had he been admitted to our councils, a permanent good feeling might have been established between the two races.'

Wiremu Tāmihana Tarapīpipi Te Waharoa was a man of peace forced into war. He lived by the principles of Te Whakapono, Te Ture, Te Aroha: be steadfast in faith in God, uphold the rule of law, show love and compassion to all.   *Evelyn Stokes*

Brown, A. N. Journal, letters and papers, 1835–1864. MS. The Elms, Tauranga

Gorst, J. E. *The Māori King.* Ed. with an introduction by K. Sinclair. Hamilton, 1959

Rickard, L. S. *Tāmihana the kingmaker.* Wellington, 1963

Taylor, R. T*he past and present of New Zealand.* London, 1868

Ward, A. 'Toa and tumuaki: contrasting leadership in the early King movements'. *Te Māori* 1, No 2 (Spring 1969): 47–51, 59

Part Two

Tāwhiao

Te Paea Tīaho

Tāmati Ngāpora

Wiremu Pātara Te Tuhi

King Tāwhiao.

Tāwhiao

?–1894

Tainui and Ngāti Mahuta leader, second Māori King, prophet

Tāwhiao, of Ngāti Mahuta in the Tainui confederation of tribes, was the son of Waikato leader Pōtatau Te Wherowhero and Whakaawi, Pōtatau's senior wife. He was born at Ōrongokoekoeā on the upper Mōkau River towards the end of the musket wars between Ngā Puhi and Waikato. It is said that he was named Tūkāroto to commemorate Pōtatau's stand at the siege of Mātakitaki pā in May 1822. Later he was baptised Matutaera (Methuselah) by the Anglican missionary Robert Burrows. In 1864 Te Ua Haumēne, the Hauhau prophet, bestowed on him the name Tāwhiao.

He was raised by his maternal grandparents. During his adolescent years, his father encouraged him to be a man of peace. He was a Christian and a student of the Bible, as well as being well versed in the ancient rites of the Tainui priesthood. In later years Tāwhiao's sayings were repeated as prophecies for the future.

His father was a renowned warrior and leader, and in 1858 was installed as the first Māori King. The King movement's supporters hoped that the position would help protect Māori land and foster unity between tribes. On Pōtatau's death in 1860 Tāwhiao became the second Māori King. His reign was to last for 34 years, through the most turbulent era of Māori–Pākehā relations.

The major issues that confronted Māori after the signing of the Treaty of Waitangi in 1840 were the desire of the growing settler population for more land, and increasing social disorganisation as a result of European contact. Within the space of a generation, Māori had moved from a world in which they were totally in control to one in which control was rapidly moving into the hands of the settlers. The wars of the 1860s in Taranaki and Waikato and the government's subsequent confiscation of Māori land saw Tāwhiao and his people rendered virtually landless and forced to retreat as wandering refugees into the heartland of Ngāti Maniapoto, now known as the King Country. As a result of the invasion of Waikato by British forces in 1863 on the pretext that the Waikato tribes were preparing to attack Auckland, Tāwhiao and his people lost over a million acres to the settler government and subsequently to the settlers themselves.

Tāwhiao assumed leadership of the King movement during this traumatic period. His travels, throughout the land of the Tainui people and beyond, brought him into contact with people desperately seeking hope and deliverance from settler encroachment. Many Māori communities have retained accounts of Tāwhiao's visits and sayings, in varying versions and with differing interpretations. The people were suffering from anxiety, deprivation, frustration and alienation. If deliverance was not to be found on earth, then perhaps assistance for Māori could be sought on another plane. A promise of salvation is encapsulated in the saying often heard on Waikato marae: 'This way of life will not continue beyond the days of my grandchildren when we shall reach salvation.' Through his reading of Scripture and discussion with early missionaries, Tāwhiao became aware that his was not a unique struggle. He believed that in time others would come to the assistance of his cause, hence his saying, 'My friends will come from the four ends of the world. They are the shoemakers, the blacksmiths and the carpenters.'

During a visit to Taranaki about 1864 Tāwhiao left one of his most enduring sayings: 'You, Taranaki, have one handle of the kit, and I, Waikato, have the other. A child will come some day and gather together its contents.' At the same time Tāwhiao made a pact with the Taranaki people that the 'kit' containing the confiscated lands of both tribes was to be held as a trust until the day when one of their own would investigate its contents; that is, seek redress for past injustices. Sir Māui Pōmare of Taranaki and Tūmate Mahuta of Waikato were later believed to have been the descendants anticipated by Tāwhiao: Pōmare used the issue of confiscation in his campaign for election to Parliament in 1911; Tūmate,

Tāwhiao's grandson and the younger brother of Te Rata, the fourth Māori King, made representations to government officials in the 1930s, concerning the injustices caused by the confiscations.

Tāwhiao was regarded as a great visionary, and had many followers. His sayings have been variously described as poropititanga, tongi and whakakitenga; all of these terms imply prophetic, visionary or prescient states of being. The years from 1864 to 1881 which he and his followers spent in isolation provided them with ample time to meditate and speculate on their fate. It was during these quiescent times that many of his sayings emerged. These sayings provided a philosophical and ideological vision from which his followers would attempt to seek salvation. Reflecting on the military defeat of his people, the land confiscations, and the defection of many Māori to Christianity and the lifestyle of the Pākehā, Tāwhiao promised that those who had remained faithful to the tenets of the King movement would be redeemed and exonerated by history. Tāwhiao and his followers saw their predicament as a dramatic parallel to the biblical exile of the children of Israel.

Tāwhiao's fundamentally pacifist nature is apparent in his renunciation of warfare between Māori and Pākehā. He said, 'Beware of being enticed to take up the sword. The result of war is that things become like decaying, old dried flax leaves. Let the person who raises war beware, for he must pay the price.' During 1875 he adopted the Pai Mārire religion – in his own version, which was called Tariao (morning star) – as the faith of the King movement. The name 'Pai Mārire' (good and gentle) was taken from a Waikato ritual chant. Tāwhiao's grand-daughter, Te Puea, ensured the continuance of Pai Mārire into modern times, recalling the story of how, just before his death, Tāwhiao told his people, 'I shall return this gift to the base of the mountains, leaving it there to lie. When you are heavily burdened, then fetch it to you.'

In the later 1860s and the 1870s a number of meetings were held between the government and Tāwhiao and his advisers, but little progress towards a reconciliation was made. In May 1878 the premier, George Grey, approached Tāwhiao with a proposal including the return of unsold lands on the west of the Waipā and Waikato rivers, land at Ngāruawāhia and in other townships, monetary aid, and rights over roads, surveys and land dealings. The thrust behind Grey's settlement was his wish to open the King Country, closed to Pākehā after the wars, so that a railway line running the length of the North Island could be built. On his council's advice Tāwhiao refused. In July 1881, however, Tāwhiao suggested a meeting with the government's representative at Alexandra (Pirongia) where he laid down his weapons, saying, 'This is the end of warfare in this land.'

While residing in Ngāti Maniapoto territory, Tāwhiao lived at various places including Tokangamutu (Te Kūiti), Hangatiki, Waitomo, Hiku-rangi (south of Pirongia Mountain) and Te Kakawa (on the shores of Aotea Harbour). Following his peace agreement with the government, he lived at Whatiwhatihoe, Maungatautari, Pukekawa and Pārāwera.

Denied the justice he sought from the New Zealand government, in 1884 Tāwhiao led a deputation to England with a petition to Queen Victoria. When he was asked the reason for his journey he replied, 'I am going to see the Queen of England, to have the Treaty of Waitangi honoured'. The petition proposed a separate Māori parliament, the appointment of a special commissioner as intermediary between Pākehā and Māori parliaments, and an independent commission of inquiry into land confiscations. At a meeting with Lord Derby, the secretary of state for the colonies, Tāwhiao acknowledged Queen Victoria's supremacy, and defined his own kingship as uniting the Māori as one people; not for purposes of separation but to claim the Queen's protection. However, Lord Derby stated that the petition had first to be referred to the New Zealand government. The New Zealand premier, Robert Stout, eventually responded to the Colonial Office by declining to discuss events preceding 1865, when the imperial government was responsible, and denying that there had been any infraction of the treaty since then. Tāwhiao's specific proposals were dismissed or ignored.

Home in Waikato, Tāwhiao sought solutions to Māori problems through the establishment of Māori institutions to deal with them. In 1885 he initiated the institution of Poukai, where the King would pay annual visits to King movement marae to encourage people to return to their home marae at least once a year. The first Poukai (originally called Puna-kai, or 'source of food') was held at Whatiwhatihoe in March 1885. It was a day for the less fortunate to be fed and entertained. The Poukai developed into an event which would later ensure direct consultation of the people with the King. In 1886 he suggested to the government that a Māori council be established, with wide-ranging powers. This was rejected, and his references to rights under the Treaty of Waitangi ignored. In the late 1880s he created his own parliament, Te Kauhanganui, at Maungākawa, to which all tribes were invited and asked to participate. However, many tribes resisted any suggestion of Tāwhiao's authority beyond his own people, and the Kotahitanga parliaments, which Tāwhiao and Te Kauhanganui supported in some measure, presented another forum for discussion of Māori concerns and communication with the government.

In the 1880s Tāwhiao's peregrinations to areas outside the King Country were significant political events in the Māori world. His personal behaviour often provoked disillusionment, even disgust, but his perceived role as a vessel of tapu, a prophet, and the King movement leader seemed able to overcome this. He was usually received with deep respect, and utmost efforts were made to entertain him and his followers royally. But his hosts did not hesitate to set bounds to his authority, and many refused to acknowledge or use his title of 'King'. Pākehā New Zealand had no wish to encourage Māori sovereignty and unity, and from the 1860s newspaper editorials and government ministers had been describing the King movement as a spent force.

Tāwhiao died on 26 August 1894 at Pārāwera. He was buried at Taupiri after a tangihanga in September which was attended by thousands. He did not live to see the fruition of his dreams for the return of Waikato land and the revival of self-sufficiency and morale among his people. Tāwhiao was close to six feet tall, and had an elaborate facial tattoo – unusual among the chiefs of his era. He had children by three wives, but a number of his other offspring were not acknowledged except within their mothers' hapū. His principal wife was Hera, the daughter of his adviser, Tāmati Ngāpora. They had three children: Tiahuia, who married Te

Tahuna Hērangi and was the mother of Te Puea; Mahuta, who succeeded Tāwhiao as King; and Te Wherowhero. Tāwhiao's other wives were Rangiaho (with whom he had two children, Pōkaia and Haunui) and Aotea: their child was Puahaere.

Tāwhiao left a legacy of religious principles from which his people would draw a future dream for Tainui: the rebirth of a self-sufficient economic base, supported by the strength and stability of the people. Native trees and foods symbolise strength and self-sufficiency in his statement: 'I shall build my own house, the ridge-pole will be of hīnau and the supporting posts of māhoe and patatē. Those who inhabit that house shall be raised on rengarenga and nurtured on kawariki.' During Tāwhiao's exile, Waikato people had reflected and focused on the powerful symbols of the King movement. The man and the vision became united, and part of the traditions and knowledge of the people. The vision is recounted and passed on to later generations at tribal hui, where it continues to be discussed and debated. *R. T. Mahuta*

Jones, P. Te H. 'Māori Kings'. In *The Māori people in the nineteen-sixties*. Ed. E. Schwimmer. Auckland, 1968
King, M. *Te Puea*. Auckland, 1977
Obit. *Auckland Star*. 27 Aug. 1894
Parsonson, A. R. 'Te mana o te Kīngitanga Māori: a study of Waikato–Ngātimaniapoto relations during the struggle for the King Country, 1878–84'. MA thesis, University of Canterbury, 1972

Te Paea Tīaho

?–1875

Tainui and Ngāti Mahuta woman of mana

Te Paea (Sophia) Tīaho, of Ngāti Mahuta, was born probably in the early 1820s in Waikato. Her father was Pōtatau Te Wherowhero, the first Māori King. Her mother was probably his senior wife, Whakaawi, but may have been Raharaha, one of his junior wives. Her siblings included Matutaera, later known as Tāwhiao, who succeeded his father as king; and Tīria, also known as Te Otaota or Mākareta.

Te Paea showed her chiefly qualities as a teenaged girl. War between the Waikato and Hawke's Bay tribes had led to the serious defeat of the latter about 1824. But by the 1830s Ngāti Te Whatuiāpiti and Ngāti Kahungunu, led by Te Pareihe, were acquiring arms and had achieved a series of victories over their other enemies. The chiefs of Waikato believed they would be the next to be attacked. Te Paea, accompanied by two other women (the daughters of Wahanui Huatare and Wiremu Tāmihana Tarapīpipi), was ordered to go to Te Pareihe as a hostage for peace.

The three women travelled to Tāmaki-makau-rau (Auckland) and then by ship to Nukutaurua on the Māhia Peninsula. Thinking that the ship was a whaling vessel, Te Pareihe's people permitted the passengers to land. Te Pareihe assembled the surrounding tribes, and Te Paea delivered Waikato's plea that peace be made. Although opposed by other chiefs Te Pareihe agreed, and instead of retaining the women as hostages or slaves he allowed Te Paea and her companions to carry the news of peace back to Waikato.

Little more is known of Te Paea until she moved from Māngere to Ngāruawāhia. The date of this is uncertain. From the outset of the King movement at Ngāruawāhia Te Paea seems to have been recognised as an influential leader. Apparently writing in the lifetime of Pōtatau Te Wherowhero, Erenora Taratoa of Ngāti Raukawa referred in a waiata to Waikato, where 'King Pōtatau, Te Paea And Matutaera ... hold sway. ... For the prestige of New Zealand'. However, Te Paea told the Reverend Arthur Purchas in 1863 that when her father had gone to Ngāruawāhia in 1858 to be installed as king, she had remained at Māngere in obedience to his wishes, and in consequence she was not present when he died in June 1860.

According to J. E. Gorst's account, on Pōtatau Te Wherowhero's death there was some difficulty finding a successor. Candidates included Wiremu Tāmihana Tarapīpipi of Ngāti Hauā, and Te Wherowhero's son, Matutaera. In Gorst's estimation the latter was regarded as weak, and his sister, Te Paea, was put forward. She was then about 35 years old, resolute and intelligent. Wiremu Tāmihana was in temporary disfavour with the King's followers because he advocated peace; after some hesitation, he declared his support for Matutaera, and Te Paea's claims were withdrawn.

Many acts of leadership during the 1860s are attributed to Te Paea. In 1862 Wiremu Nēra Te Awaitaia of Raglan tried to build a road from that place to the Waipā River. This was regarded with deep suspicion by the King's supporters, as the road would be a potential route for the conquest of Waikato by government troops. As a relative of Te Awaitaia, Te Paea was able to intervene. With her own hands she pulled up the survey pegs that marked his proposed route.

Te Paea's influence was usually employed in favour of moderation and peace. The government's plan to establish a school at Te Awamutu, where young men would be trained as loyal servants of the government, together with the establishment of a bullet-proof steamer on the Waikato River, were regarded by the Kingites as hostile moves. Difficulties arose over the purchase of timber for the school buildings, and when a faction of Ngāti Maniapoto carted away the sawn timber a stormy meeting followed. Gorst, the resident magistrate for Waikato, insisted on its return. Te Paea, while visiting Kihikihi, asked that the disputed timber be gifted to her, which, given her status, was a request impossible to refuse. She then presented it to Gorst. This ended the immediate difficulty, and for a time seemed to promise peace in Waikato.

At about this time the King movement became divided over the advisability of converting to Catholicism. Some were drawn to that religion because it professed no allegiance to the Queen. Te Paea opposed Catholicism. She and other leaders presided over a dinner given for all the local Europeans at Rangiaowhia (Rangiaohia) to commemorate the accession of the King, and a day or two afterwards she took part in a friendly visit to Te Awamutu which resulted in an invitation to the governor to visit Waikato.

As events drew nearer to war, Governor George Grey made an unannounced visit to Ngāruawāhia, at the beginning of January 1863. King Tāwhiao was absent, and Grey was welcomed by Te Paea. She asked Grey why he did not make the surprise complete by cutting down the King's flagstaff; she would have refused him nothing. At Kihikihi in April Te Paea told Rewi Maniapoto that the mission station at Te Awamutu had been entrusted to her safe-keeping for the missionaries until more peaceful times. Rewi and his people had wanted to occupy the mission buildings, but Rewi promised to respect Te Paea's wishes. At Ngāruawāhia, Te Paea went into the chiefs' rūnanga, which was discussing whether to defend Te Awamutu from Ngāti Maniapoto, and harangued the chiefs in the cause of peace.

Te Paea and Pātara Te Tuhi, the King's adviser, made further endeavours to prevent violence, but their efforts were overtaken by events. They then warned Gorst and other officials, settlers and missionaries to leave Waikato because Tāwhiao could not protect them from Ngāti Maniapoto. In consequence, most had left by the end of June 1863. Te Paea had planned to return to Māngere to live, as her father had wished, but, she told Purchas in April, she had been forced to stay in Waikato because of the unsettled state of the people. She would go if they continued to disregard her father's behest to 'Live in peace with the Pākehā'. The outbreak of war in July prevented her from making the move.

Nothing was recorded about Te Paea during the war years, and few official mentions were made of her in the time before her death. It is clear that she continued to be regarded as one of the principal King movement leaders at Kāwhia, and at Te Kūiti, where she lived. The Waikato chief Te Wheoro recorded in 1870 that it was her decision that would permit or block the opening up of the Ōhinemuri goldfield. Europeans sometimes referred to her as 'Princess Sophia'. She died on 22 January 1875. Her tangihanga was held at Tāwhiao's residence at Waitomo, near Te Kūiti. She had no issue.   *Angela Ballara*

Appendices to the Journals of the House of Representatives (New Zealand). 1863, E–1
Gorst, J. E. *The Māori King*. London, 1864

Tāmati Ngāpora

?–1885

Tainui and Ngāti Mahuta leader, lay preacher, assessor,
adviser to the Māori King

Ngāpora was born early in the nineteenth century. He belonged to Ngāti Mahuta of Waikato. His parents were Hore and Kahurimu. He was the nephew of Te Rauangaanga and a cousin of Pōtatau Te Wherowhero. He was said to have fought as a young man at the defence of Mātakitaki pā against Ngā Puhi in 1822. He may have taken part in the wars fought in the 1820s and 1830s by Waikato against Taranaki tribes and Te Arawa of Rotorua. He and his family became Christians, and he took the name Tāmati (Thomas). His wife was named Hera. They had at least one daughter, also named Hera.

In 1848 Ngāpora wrote to Governor George Grey to express his concern about the decreasing power of chiefly authority in Māori society and its consequences for law and order. His letter was passed on to Earl Grey, the secretary of state for the colonies, whose solution to the problem was to suggest that chiefly authority be upheld by granting chiefs land titles and local jurisdiction. This suggestion was not taken up by the governor, however.

Ngāpora and many Ngāti Mahuta, including Te Wherowhero, left Waikato and went to live at Māngere. They agreed in 1849 to provide military assistance to protect Auckland. Ngāpora was an Anglican lay preacher, and also an assessor, or assistant to the resident magistrate in the affairs of the local Māori community. He was a strong supporter of temperance. He also built a stone church at his village of Ihumātao, near Māngere.

In the 1850s, when the King movement rose to prominence as an

Tāmati Ngāpora. Portrait by Gottfried Lindauer.

attempt to consolidate Māori authority and halt land sales, Ngāpora's inclination was initially against an intertribal Māori kingship. However, when Te Wherowhero was installed as King and returned to live in Waikato, Ngāpora remained at Māngere to act as the King movement's representative to the governor. In 1861, when Sir George Grey returned to New Zealand as governor, Ngāpora arranged for leaders of the King movement to meet him. At the meeting Rewi Maniapoto insisted on recognition of the Māori King's independence, which Grey would not grant. In 1863 the dispute over sovereignty moved towards war. Ngāpora warned the governor that war parties were gathering to attack the government outpost of Te Ia (Havelock, near Mercer), and that there were plans for a surprise attack on Auckland. In July 1863 Māori north of the Mangatāwhiri River were required to give an oath of allegiance to Queen Victoria, or leave for Waikato. Ngāpora considered this requirement to be insulting, and refused the oath. Soldiers looted Māori property and an atmosphere of open hostility developed. Disillusioned, Ngāpora returned to Waikato. Meanwhile, on 12 July, Lieutenant General Duncan Cameron and British troops had crossed the Mangatāwhiri River to invade Waikato. Although he did not take part in the fighting in Waikato, after the war and the confiscation of Waikato land Ngāpora went into exile in the King Country with Te Wherowhero's son, Tāwhiao.

Ngāpora lived at Tokangamutu (Te Kūiti) in the territory of Ngāti Maniapoto, and changed his name to Manuhiri (guest), to reflect his exile. Te Wherowhero had proposed that Ngāpora should succeed him but others, including Wiremu Tāmihana Tarapīpipi, had preferred Tāwhiao. Ngāpora became Tāwhiao's closest adviser, and his daughter, Hera, became the King's wife. His close connections with the King gave Ngāpora great influence within the King movement. He became, for a time, a follower of Pai Mārire. However, he tried to stop the war party of Ngāti Maniapoto which destroyed the government blockhouse of Pukearuhe (White Cliffs) in North Taranaki in February 1869, and was against the King movement's forces joining Te Kooti in renewed war with the government.

The boundaries of the King Country were still closed to Europeans in

1879, preventing the construction of the railway line south from Hamilton. Rewi Maniapoto wanted to use the government's need for access as a means to negotiate the return of some Waikato land, but Ngāpora and other Waikato counsellors to the King opposed any peace settlement without the return of all confiscated lands. They saw Grey, now premier, as the author of their misfortunes. At a meeting at Hikurangi, near Kāwhia, in 1878, Grey offered the King movement 500 acres at Ngāruawāhia and the return of all unsold confiscated land west of the Waikato River. This was rejected as inadequate by Ngāpora and other Waikato leaders. At a meeting with Grey at Te Kōpua the following year, Ngāpora flourished a copy of Grey's proclamation of 1863 expelling Māori from South Auckland, and demanded the return of all confiscated land.

In 1881 Tāwhiao formally submitted to the government at Alexandra (Pirongia). He was accompanied by over 500 warriors, and by Ngāpora and other leaders. Ngāpora continued to live at Whatiwhatihoe, the royal village in the King Country, where he died on 5 August 1885. He was believed to be about 80 years of age. Rewi stayed with him during his last days and Tāwhiao came to see him before he died.   *Steven Oliver*

Cowan, J. *The New Zealand wars*. 2 vols. Wellington, 1922–23
Gorst, J. E. *The Māori King*. London, 1864
Martin, M. A. *Our Maoris*. London, 1884

Wiremu Pātara Te Tuhi

?–1910

*Tainui and Ngāti Mahuta leader, newspaper editor, warrior,
secretary to the Māori King*

Te Tuhi was born in Waikato. He belonged to Ngāti Mahuta. His father
was Paratene Te Maioha, a cousin of Pōtatau Te Wherowhero, the first
Māori King. Te Tuhi was a second cousin of Tāwhiao, Te Wherowhero's
successor, and served him as editor, warrior, secretary and adviser.

In his youth Te Tuhi attended mission schools and lived for a time at
Kāwhia. He appears to have become a Christian, taking Wiremu Pātara
(William Butler) as his baptismal name. In 1856 Iwikau Te Heuheu
Tūkino III held a meeting at Pūkawa where it was decided to offer the
Māori kingship to Te Wherowhero. Te Tuhi, then known as Taieti,
attended as Te Wherowhero's representative.

In 1859 two Waikato Māori, Wiremu Toetoe and Hēmara Te Rerehau,
travelled to Austria on the frigate *Novara*, and were trained in printing
techniques at the state printing house in Vienna. As a parting gift, in May
1860 Archduke Maximilian gave them a printing press, which was shipped
to Ngāruawāhia. Late in 1861 the press was used to print a newspaper,
which carried the proclamations of Tāwhiao, who had succeeded his
father, Te Wherowhero, as King, and news of the King movement to its
adherents. Pātara Te Tuhi became the editor and principal writer of the
newspaper, which was named *Te Hōkioi e Rere Atu Nā*, after a mythical bird
which was flying to spread the news. Through the newspaper he argued for
an interpretation of the Treaty of Waitangi that would limit the sovereignty of the colonial government over Māori. He argued, for instance,
that the presence of a government steamer on the Waikato River, without
the permission of the Māori owners of the river, violated the treaty.

Wiremu Pātara Te Tuhi.

Early in 1863 the King movement warned Te Wheoro, a government supporter, not to proceed with the construction of a fortified constabulary station at Te Kohekohe, on the west bank of the Waikato River, south of Meremere. Te Wheoro ignored the warnings, and proceeded to have timber prepared and carpenters brought from Auckland. Supporters of the King, led by Wī Kumete Te Whitiora, threw the timber into the river and made the carpenters flee. The timber was rafted down the Waikato River to the government redoubt at Te Ia (Havelock, near Mercer), at the junction with the Mangatāwhiri River. Pātara Te Tuhi later said that it was he who first proposed sending the timber back to Te Ia, but he had not anticipated the violence that would follow.

In February 1863 the government set up a rival Māori newspaper at Te Awamutu, edited by John Gorst. *Te Pīhoihoi Mokemoke i Runga i te Tuanui*, taking its name from Psalm 102:7 ('I watch, and am as a sparrow alone upon the house-top'), put forward Governor George Grey's argument that there could not be two governments in authority over one country. The paper's criticism of the King so incensed Ngāti Mahuta and the King movement's supporters that on 24 March 1863 80 armed warriors, led by Rewi Maniapoto and Āporo Taratutu, entered the town of Te Awamutu. Āporo led them to the office of the government newspaper, where the printing press, paper and copies of the fifth (and last) issue of *Te Pīhoihoi* were seized. Gorst was ordered to leave Te Awamutu, and was accommodated by Pātara Te Tuhi in the printing house at Ngāruawāhia on his way back to Auckland. The expulsion was a challenge to the authority of Grey. On Pātara's advice, Tāwhiao condemned Rewi's actions, and ordered him to return the press and to leave to the King the question of the presence of the governor's official in Waikato. Various factions developed in the King movement, with Ngāti Maniapoto and some lower Waikato chiefs advocating war, and Ngāti Hauā and Waikato wanting to reduce tensions with the government. Pātara Te Tuhi and others successfully opposed Rewi's plan to take a fleet of canoes down the Waikato River to attack Te Ia.

War began, however, on 12 July 1863, when Lieutenant General Duncan Cameron and British troops crossed the Mangatāwhiri River.

Te Hōkioi ceased publication and the press was abandoned (it is now in the Te Awamutu Museum). Pātara Te Tuhi fought against the British all through the campaign in Waikato, and went into exile with Tāwhiao in 1864. The King and his followers remained in isolation in the King Country for nearly 20 years. In May 1878 Pātara Te Tuhi spoke at a meeting at Hikurangi, near Kāwhia, at which Grey, now premier, was present. He told Grey that the King movement was reluctant to begin negotiations with the government until the confiscation of Waikato lands had been discussed. This issue stalemated negotiations for a number of years. In 1881 Tāwhiao formally submitted to the government at Alexandra (Pirongia), and in January 1882 Pātara Te Tuhi accompanied the King on a tour of the North Island. On their arrival in Auckland Pātara delivered the King's prepared speech to the crowd attending the civic welcome.

In 1884 Pātara Te Tuhi went to England with Tāwhiao, as the King's assistant and secretary. After returning to New Zealand he lived at Māngere, near his brother, Hōnana Te Maioha. His portrait was painted by C. F. Goldie and a number of photographs were taken of him, showing him to be an imposing figure with a fully tattooed face. He represented Tāwhiao at an intertribal conference at Ōrākei in 1889 and was responsible for issuing proclamations for Mahuta, who succeeded Tāwhiao as King in 1894.

Pātara Te Tuhi was admired by both Māori and Pākehā for his shrewdness and his good nature. John Gorst, his rival editor in Waikato, praised his 'wit and ability', and was pleased to meet him again on a visit to New Zealand in 1906. He died at Māngere on 2 July 1910 and was said to be aged 85 or 86. He was buried at Taupiri, near the Waikato River.

Steven Oliver

Cowan, J. *The New Zealand wars.* Vol. 1, *1845-64.* Wellington, 1922
Gorst, J. E. *The Māori King.* London, 1864
Kelly, L. G. *Tainui.* Wellington, 1949
Obit. *New Zealand Free Lance.* 9 July 1910

Part Three

Mahuta

Hēnare Kaihau

Tupu Atanatiu Taingākawa Te Waharoa

T.T. Rāwhiti

King Mahuta.

Mahuta

1854/55?–1912

Tainui and Ngāti Mahuta leader, third Māori King, politician

Mahuta Tāwhiao of Ngāti Mahuta was born at Whatiwhatihoe, Waikato, probably in 1854 or 1855. He was the eldest son of Tāwhiao, the second Māori King, and his senior wife, Hera. She was the daughter of Tāmati Ngāpora (Manuhiri) of Ngāti Mahuta, Tāwhiao's adviser, and his wife, Hera. Mahuta's elder sister was Tiahuia, the mother of Te Puea Hērangi. Mahuta had many half-brothers and half-sisters from his father's other marriages and connections.

The family's selection by many central North Island tribes to serve as kings reflected its senior lines of descent and important kin connections to other tribes. Mahuta could trace his descent from the crews of Tainui, Te Arawa, Mātaatua, Tokomaru, Kurahaupō, Tākitimu and other canoes. It also reflected the family's early wealth: fertile lands on the banks of the Waikato River, itself a source of food, were complemented by nearby forests and lakes. Since part of the king's role was similar to that of the traditional ariki, it was essential for him to have the means for ample hospitality. The course of Mahuta's reign was shaped by this expectation; the established sequence of hui and ritual events, the manifestations of the functioning King movement, had to be supplied by a people impoverished by the confiscation of their lands.

Mahuta grew up during the wars of the 1860s and the period of isolation that followed. As a result, although trained in Waikato tradition and whakapapa, and in the composition of waiata, he received little if any European education. He spoke almost no English, and his handwriting remained shaky and unformed throughout his life. As an adult he was his father's heir apparent, and made use of the literacy and numeracy skills of others such as T. T. Rāwhiti and Hēnare Kaihau to an extent that left him dependent on their services and integrity. Partly for this reason, Mahuta has often been seen as a figurehead within his own kingdom, pushed this way and that by strong leaders of different factions. But he had a clear perception of his role as the custodian of Tāwhiao's political and religious legacy, and often set the factional leaders against each other, achieving his own ends through the blunting of theirs.

Probably in the 1870s, Mahuta married Te Marae, a woman of strong, independent character who became a King movement leader in her own right. Mahuta and Te Marae had five surviving sons: Te Rata (eventually the fourth King), Taipū, Tūmate, Tonga and Te Rauangaanga.

When Tāwhiao died in August 1894, Tupu Taingākawa Te Waharoa, known as the kingmaker, anointed Mahuta as the third King while his father's body lay in state at Taupiri. Mahuta is deemed to have become King on 14 September 1894. On 15 September, accompanied by other members of the royal family, he made a formal entrance into the house of his parliament, Te Kauhanganui, and was seated on his father's throne. His younger brother, Te Wherowhero Tāwhiao, announced that Mahuta was to be known as 'King Tāwhiao III', a title later used on some occasions. He was also known as Kiingi Tāwhiao Te Aaha-o-te-rangi. Mahuta spoke, promising to hold on to Tāwhiao's sayings and teachings. Out on the marae three volleys were fired in honour of the new King.

Allegiance to Mahuta, based on that given to Tāwhiao, was regarded partly as a covenant with him to hold the lands of those tribes acknow-ledging the authority of the Māori King. The movement had attracted its greatest support in the 1860s; even in 1881 Wahanui Huatare had been able to plant 34 poles at Hikurangi representing supporting tribes, in-cluding Taranaki and Whanganui tribes, Ngāti Awa, Ngāti Kahungunu, some Te Arawa and even one small group of Ngā Puhi. But the erosion of this support had been rapid in the 1880s, and some tribes only nominally acknowledged his authority. Of these, many had abandoned the full Kīngitanga programme: they were not withholding their lands from the colony's land courts and were permitting government committees to be set up in their regions according to legislative provision. Ngāti Maniapoto had allowed the main trunk railway to proceed.

But although the kingdom was shrinking in size and influence, in many ways it was assuming a more formal organisational shape. When Mahuta succeeded to the throne, many of the plans of Te Kauhanganui were being formalised for the first time and mana motuhake (local autonomy) was being realised to some extent. Soon after Mahuta's succession, Taingākawa, as leader of the King's government, announced the setting up of the kingdom's own courts for land, civil and criminal cases. Judges, registrars, police and clerks were appointed; dog taxes and fines for non-payment were organised. A minister of lands was appointed, to whom the kingdom's subjects could apply if they wished to lease out their lands. Land court block hearings were 'gazetted' in *Te Paki o Matariki*, the King movement's newspaper. Spokesmen were appointed to mediate tribal disputes. There was also a plan to set up King movement schools.

These plans of 1894 and 1895 were not Mahuta's personal work, but he encouraged and endorsed them by his presence at hui at which they were adopted, and by his constant exhortations to the members of Te Kauhanganui. The plans foundered through official resistance to King movement assumption of government or local government functions, and also through lack of means. Mahuta's kingdom had none but moral pressure to exert; without the power to enforce its taxes and fines it was without funds to pay its officers and finance its schools and had to depend on traditional, voluntary support.

These weaknesses and the desperate state of his people forced Mahuta to attempt to find redress for the Waikato confiscations of the 1860s. These were the root of a deepening economic crisis which was producing a vicious cycle of poverty, disease and depopulation at a time when Māori in some other areas were beginning to recover. Some tribes were coping by selling or leasing land; Mahuta's people had none to spare. Kauri gum and rabbit skins provided income for some, but both sources had ceased by 1903. Flax milling required back-breaking labour in swamps and was plagued by fluctuating demand. Mahuta's people were surviving by raising a few sheep and through subsistence farming on their remaining lands. In an effort to end the downward spiral Mahuta consulted a tohunga, who advised that the bodies of King Pōtatau and his ancestors be exhumed and reburied on Taupiri Mountain, a ceremony carried out on 23 January 1903.

In 1895 Mahuta briefly considered a union with Te Kotahitanga, the movement for an independent Māori parliament. United Māori pressure on the government might produce redress for grievances. Representatives arrived from the fourth parliamentary session in Rotorua, armed with deeds setting out the aims of Te Kotahitanga to which they hoped he would give his agreement. Mahuta sanctioned the setting up of a committee including Tūreiti Te Heuheu Tūkino and T. T. Rāwhiti to explore ways of uniting the efforts of both groups, but Taingākawa quashed this development by setting up a rival deed, later known as Mahuta's deed, for King movement followers to sign. It was circulated in Waikato and on the Kāwhia coast, and signed – it was claimed – by 5,000.

Eventually Mahuta was forced to turn to the colonial government for help. At a meeting at Waahi pā, Huntly, on 4 April 1898, Premier Richard Seddon brought up the idea of Mahuta accepting a seat on the Legislative Council. Some leading King movement supporters warned that the government would expect Mahuta to abandon his independence, but negotiations proceeded. Encouraged by his reception at Waahi, in 1900 Seddon worked on detailed proposals suggesting a measure of Māori self-government and bills to enable Māori to manage and conserve the remnants of their land and to return some of the confiscated land. The proposal to return land was later replaced with an offer to talk in general terms about landless Māori. Mahuta was also offered a seat in the cabinet, so that he could deliberate over all matters affecting Māori. An offer of a yearly pension was replaced with a promise to discuss how the dignity of Mahuta's high position was to be maintained. The amended version was sent to Mahuta on 31 August 1900.

It must have seemed to Mahuta that he was being handed, all at once, recognition, redress and future sustenance for his people. After a flurry of telegrams, he met Seddon in Wellington on 17 September. Mahuta told Seddon that he would accept his offers after discussion with his people.

He said that at the same time they should settle the boundaries of the Waikato District Māori Land Council, planned to be set up under the Māori Lands Administration Act 1900; Mahuta wanted its district to include most of the central North Island. When he laid the offers before his people and Te Kauhanganui, opposition to the plan centred on concessions Mahuta would be expected to make and the fate of the independent Māori kingdom. Mahuta asked Seddon to hold over the proposal for a while.

Seddon's legislation of that year met with mixed success in Waikato. Although implementation of the Māori Councils Act 1900 did not get off the ground there, with Mahuta's encouragement the Waikato District Māori Land Council held its first sitting on 15 April 1903 at his settlement at Waahi. Nearly 300 Māori attended, and on 16 April Mahuta brought the first case, asking the council to recommend the removal of restrictions on alienation of land he and his wife owned at Kāwhia.

Encouraged by this sign of Mahuta's support for land settlement, Seddon renewed his offers; Mahuta accepted, and was appointed to the Legislative Council and sworn in as a member of the Executive Council on 22 May 1903. His appointment was widely regarded as the end of Waikato Māori isolation and intransigence; in fact it was the beginning of a short-lived experiment in co-operation with Pākehā authority.

Mahuta's appointments were attended by controversy. The governor, Lord Ranfurly, approved of his appointment to the Legislative Council, but reserved his opinion about the Executive Council post because of doubts about Mahuta's character and his reported drinking. Seddon claimed that the appointment was essential because nothing had been done in the King Country to place Māori land in the hands of a Māori land council for settlement purposes. The owners of these lands regarded Mahuta as their head, and would follow his direction. Seddon canvassed support against Ranfurly from his ministers; Sir Joseph Ward waffled, but the minister of native affairs, James Carroll, perhaps unaware that the kingship had been temporarily entrusted to Mahuta's younger brother, Te Wherowhero Tāwhiao, predicted that Ranfurly would give way once it was made clear to him that by accepting these posts Mahuta would be

Mahuta, family and supporters at Parliament, probably in 1903.

abandoning his kingship. As he was bound to do, Ranfurly accepted his ministers' advice, although criticism continued inside and outside Parliament.

Mahuta's lack of English made it difficult for him to contribute in the Executive Council, but for some years, in spite of the lack of printed translations of bills, he coped with the Legislative Council. Liberal party colleagues expected him to endorse their land policies in the House, but far from feeling grateful to them, Mahuta was soon disillusioned about the potential of his role. He deplored, like other Māori members, the fact that measures important to Māori were put off until the end of the session and the last hour of the day. His amendments in 1903 to a bill amending the Māori Councils Act 1900 and to the Native Land Rating Bill in 1904 were defeated. He pointed out that Māori landowners were restricted by legislation from dealing with their own lands, and thus from getting some return with which to pay the rates. Constant themes in his speeches were that confiscation of Māori land by rating, by forced land settlement or in any other way was contrary to the Treaty of Waitangi, and that if Māori were empowered to deal with their own lands, they would soon dispel the idea that they were lazy. He did not oppose settlement by Pākehā on leased Māori lands, but in 1907 he asked why it was that legislation did not allow Māori to apply to the Government Advances to Settlers Office for cheap mortgage finance.

Disillusioned by the powerlessness of his position, Mahuta did not speak in the Legislative Council after 1907, although he continued to attend sessions until his term ended in 1910. He had been dropped from the Executive Council after the reshuffle following the death of Seddon in 1906.

In 1907 he turned to two new schemes. The first involved the establishment of a renewed Māori parliamentary movement. The idea was abandoned when other tribes were unwilling to be led by the King movement. Mahuta endorsed Taingākawa's attempts to set up a new petition for redress of grievances under the Treaty of Waitangi, but seemed to have more hope in his second scheme, the establishment of a new centre for the kingdom at Taupiri. He believed that the government was going to help him by buying out the Pākehā settlers at Taupiri in exchange for land at Aotea, and he planned to present it with an additional 5,000 acres to pay for the necessary surveying. He wanted to establish a new settlement and township to be occupied and worked by Māori, although he did not exclude the lease of some land to Pākehā. In the event, Mahuta's plans, which followed Tāwhiao's wish to re-establish the kingdom at Ngāruawāhia, were not accomplished during his lifetime. But he did purchase a site at Ngāruawāhia for the parliament house, and set aside money for its construction.

Mahuta had been referred to as 'King Mahuta' by his supporters during his Legislative Council term, and officially resumed the kingship on 21 May 1910. The last two years of his life were filled with trouble. He began to have increasing doubts about the direction in which Taingākawa was taking the King movement; his relationship with Te Marae had become fraught with suspicion; and at the same time it was becoming clear that Hēnare Kaihau was responsible for the loss, through bad investments, of

King movement funds that had come from Mahuta's sales and leases. When Māui Pōmare of Ngāti Mutunga, a Taranaki tribe, sought Waikato support for his parliamentary candidacy on a platform of seeking redress for the Waikato and Taranaki confiscations, Mahuta's position was difficult; Taingākawa had, through the pages of *Te Paki o Matariki*, publicly committed him to the continued support of Kaihau as MP for Western Māori, even as late as November 1911. At the same time Pōmare, a descendant of Te Rauparaha, had reminded him of the traditional debt incurred from the time Te Rauparaha saved Pōtatau Te Wherowhero from certain death after the battle of Motunui in 1822. Mahuta's son, Te Rata, and his niece, Te Puea Hērangi, were reflecting his wishes in covertly or overtly encouraging Pōmare's candidacy.

Mahuta's photograph, published in *Te Puke ki Hikurangi* after his death, shows him with dark hair, heavy moustache, and an intelligent, slightly despondent gaze. He died at Waahi on 9 November 1912. Hēnare Kaihau and Pēpene Eketone were in charge of the arrangements for the tangihanga. They decided that his body should lie in state for a month to permit homage to be paid to it by all the King movement tribes, a duty shared by thousands. He was buried on Taupiri Mountain.

Angela Ballara

Jones, P. Te H. 'Māori Kings'. In *The Māori people in the nineteen-sixties*. Ed. E. Schwimmer. Auckland, 1968
King, M. *Te Puea*. Auckland, 1977
Mahuta, R. 'The Māori King movement today'. In *Tihe mauri ora*. Ed. M. King. [Wellington], 1978
Obit. *Te Puke ki Hikurangi*. 21 Nov. 1912: 3
'Te Whakaarahanga o Mahuta Tāwhiao hei Kiingi'. *Te Paki o Matariki*. 15 Sept. 1894: 1

Hēnare Kaihau
1854-60?–1920

Ngāti Te Ata leader, politician, adviser to the Māori King

Hēnare Kaihau was born probably between 1854 and 1860 at Waiuku, on the southern Manukau Harbour. He was the son of Ngāti Te Ata chief Aihepene (Ahipene) Kaihau, who also had tribal affiliations with Ngāti Urupikia, Ngāti Kahukōkā and Ngāti Tīpā. Hēnare's mother's name was Rangipūkoru. Aihepene Kaihau was superintendent of police for the King movement rūnanga in 1858, and between 1862 and 1880 was a Native Department assessor at Waiuku. Little is known of Hēnare's personal life except that he married at least twice, and possibly six times, and from his second marriage had six daughters and two sons. His second wife, Louisa Flavell, also known as Maewa, was a composer to whom the words of the farewell song 'Haere rā', internationally known as 'Now is the hour', have been attributed.

Hēnare Kaihau attended Robert and Beatrice Maunsell's school at Kōhanga only briefly. He acquired a vast knowledge of tribal history and whakapapa, and later in Parliament he was to speak only in Māori. By his mid 20s he had become interested in Māori politics. He was associated with the Māori parliament movement, and was a staunch supporter of the King movement, becoming the principal adviser to Mahuta, the Māori King.

In 1884 and 1886 he stood unsuccessfully for Parliament in the Western Māori electorate. Success came in 1896 when, as the first candidate supported by the King movement, he was elected MHR for Western Māori. One of his first tasks in Parliament was to introduce in August 1898 the Māori Council Constitution Bill, which provided for a form of

Māori self-government. A Māori council of 56 members would assume full power over Māori land and fishing grounds, supplanting the Native Land Court and settling all disputes relating to Māori land. The other Māori members of the House supported the principle of the bill but objected to the clause which stated that the mana of the council was to be vested in Mahuta for life and to descend to his lawful successors. The bill was discharged before its second reading.

Throughout his 15 years in Parliament Kaihau spoke on many issues concerning Māori people, always referring to the Treaty of Waitangi as a basis for their rights. The right to fish in traditional fishing grounds and to hunt native birds without restrictions must be preserved, he argued, for these foods were the staple diet of the Māori. He believed it important that Māori have a European-style education from properly trained teachers, and argued that they should then be given equal opportunity of employment in government departments.

He gave most of his attention, however, to the issue of Māori land. Deeply concerned about the effects of land confiscation in Waikato in particular, Kaihau lamented what he saw as unkept promises made by Premier Richard Seddon and Native Minister James Carroll to deal with this issue, and repeatedly reminded the government of this obligation. He argued vehemently against a number of the Māori land bills introduced into the House between 1897 and 1910. The most controversial of these was the Māori Lands Administration Bill, which was passed in October 1900. Kaihau at first believed that the bill would benefit Māori people by giving them greater control over their land, through the institution of district land councils. However, it soon became apparent that the act further restricted Māori initiative in dealing with their land, and he argued for its repeal.

In 1903 Kaihau took a seat on the Waikato District Māori Land Council, having been persuaded by James Carroll. But the results of the Māori Lands Administration Act 1900 and the unwillingness of the government to make land laws more equitable hardened him against future land legislation. He argued passionately that these laws were trampling Māori rights and mana that had been guaranteed to them

Hēnare Kaihau.

under the Treaty of Waitangi. By 1910 these rights had effectively been taken away. Disillusioned and frustrated by the lack of commitment to Māori issues, by 1905 Kaihau spoke mostly to the Māori land bills and took his seat in Parliament only when such legislation was introduced. He did not speak in the House at all in 1906, 1908 and 1909.

During this period he turned his attention to the idea of re-establishing a Māori parliament, following the decline of the Kotahitanga movement of the 1890s. The new parliament was to be centred on Mahuta and his pā at Waahi. The aim was to rally all Māori leaders, devise a plan of self-determination and fight unjust land laws. Large meetings were held in 1907, but they failed to overcome divisions within the King movement and differences with tribes outside it.

In 1908 the Waikato leaders acted by themselves. Mahuta wanted to buy back confiscated land at Taupiri and Ngāruawāhia where he would establish a township and parliament. Money was raised through the sale and lease of land. Some was invested by Kaihau in Auckland land companies and some placed in trust funds in Kaihau's name. By 1911 the companies had collapsed and over £50,000 of King movement money had been lost.

The failure of these investments coincided with charges of impropriety brought against Kaihau in Parliament. On 12 October 1910 John Hine, the member for Stratford, laid charges of corruption against several members. Kaihau was accused of having accepted money from electors for his work on petitions, and of receiving payment for setting up land sales: while he urged his people to hold on to their lands, he assisted those who were determined to sell. In his defence Kaihau stated that he had been working in the capacity of a licensed agent, and that lawyers and others in the House did similar work for their clients and constituents. He was found 'guilty of impropriety in the execution of his office'. The Speaker, however, observed that because 'the honourable member is a Native, and . . . does not speak our language', and 'our Standing Orders are not translated into the Māori language', he may not have been 'aware that he was doing what was improper.' No penalty was imposed.

In September 1911 Kaihau was granted 14 days' leave of absence from

Parliament for health reasons; he had been suffering for some time from gout and rheumatic fever. Knowledge of his bad investments came to Mahuta just before the 1911 general election. Accusations had also been made that Kaihau had appropriated trust fund money for his own use. Mahuta subsequently transferred his allegiance to Māui Pōmare, and Pōmare defeated Kaihau at the election by 565 votes. Kaihau tried in 1919 to regain the seat, but without success. He died at Waiuku on 20 May the following year.

Hēnare Kaihau was a man of imposing presence. A large man (weighing 20 stone), he was 'a Hercules in strength and stature', in the words of the prime minister, William Massey, 'and a man with a very great deal of mental ability.' He was a master of political rhetoric, but was also described as 'extraordinarily good-natured and genial'. He has been remembered primarily for the loss of King movement money and the charge of political impropriety brought against him. However, these incidents should not overshadow his vision of Māori self-determination and his effort to unite the King and Kotahitanga movements to this end. His cry – 'give into the hands of the Māori people the power to administer their own affairs; cease to tie up the hands and feet of individuals owning the land' – should have been an important foundation for later demands for Māori self-determination.

The cyclopedia of New Zealand. Vol. 2. Christchurch, 1902
King, M. Te Puea. Auckland, 1977
New Zealand Parliamentary Debates. House of Representatives, 29 June 1920
Williams, J. A. Politics of the New Zealand Māori. Seattle, 1969

Tupu Taingākawa.

Tupu Atanatiu Taingākawa Te Waharoa
1844/45?–1929

Ngāti Hauā leader, kingmaker, King movement leader

Tupu Atanatiu Taingākawa Te Waharoa was the second son of Wiremu Tāmihana Tarapīpipi Te Waharoa and Pare Te Kanawa (Wikitōria). They belonged to Ngāti Hauā, but also had links with Ngāti Hinepare (a hapu of Ngāti Kauwhata) and Ngāti Hikairo. Taingākawa was probably born in 1844 or 1845, at either Te Tāpiri, near Matamata, or Maungākawa, overlooking the Thames (Waihou) valley. He had an elder brother, Hōtene Tāmihana Te Waharoa, usually known as Hote. There were two sisters: Hārete Tāmihana Te Waharoa and Te Raumako, also known as Te Reo. In his youth Taingākawa was known as Tana Te Waharoa or Tana Taingākawa Te Waharoa; he was later known as Tupu Taingākawa. Taingākawa may have attended the schools built by his father at Te Tāpiri and Pēria, and may also have attended mission schools.

During Taingākawa's teens and early adult years his people were living in turmoil. Under his father's leadership Ngāti Hauā had enthusiastically accepted the benefits of literacy, Christianity, agriculture and trading; Europeans regarded them as a progressive people. But political and land pressures led Wiremu Tāmihana to associate himself with the King movement in order to oppose European encroachment. Wars in Taranaki and Waikato followed, and by the time of his death late in 1866 many settlers regarded him as a rebel, the architect of an alliance designed to drive Europeans from the North Island.

Although Hote was the elder son and continued to be regarded as a chief by his own people, from 1867 Taingākawa took on a leadership role and was seen by the colonial authorities as his father's heir. His advice to the Tauranga chiefs to join the King's followers inside the aukati (King movement boundary) and his attempts to mediate between the government and Te Kooti in the early 1870s were regarded with suspicion. In 1871 Taingākawa was classed as one of the 'Ngāti Hauā Hauhaus', and his attempts at *rapprochement* were regarded as insincere.

Taingākawa probably attended an important hui near Maungatautari in June 1871, at which King movement leaders invited Ngāti Hauā to come inland and join the King's party, and promoted the policy of isolation from Pākehā. Ngāti Hauā's response was divided: some were enthusiastic supporters of the King movement; others were neutral; still others were definitely opposed. About 1873 Hote and Taingākawa took their section of Ngāti Hauā to live at Te Kūiti, then the centre of the King movement. Constantly harassed by Tāmati Ngāpora, chief adviser to the Māori King Tāwhiao Te Wherowhero, they returned to Wharepapa in 1875. From this time for a considerable period Taingākawa was relatively obscure. For nearly 20 years he was merely the son of a great father and one among the leaders of Ngāti Hauā.

Nevertheless, he remained an important supporter of the King movement, aiding Tāwhiao in his efforts to maintain authority over Ngāti Maniapoto, in whose territory he was then living. In 1884 Tāwhiao petitioned the British government for an inquiry into land confiscation, Māori self-determination, breaches of the Treaty of Waitangi, and other matters. A non-committal response was received in 1885 and discussed at a series of meetings. Taingākawa was a member of a deputation which, on 7 April 1886, interviewed the governor over the issues raised.

During the 1880s Rewi Maniapoto, Wahanui Huatare and other Ngāti Maniapoto leaders edged their people out from under Tāwhiao's protecting shade and rejected his isolationism. From 1886 Tāwhiao turned to new methods to unite Māori under his leadership. In 1889 he moved from Ngāti Maniapoto territory to Pukekawa near Mercer, and travelled about raising support for a parliament, called Te Kauhanganui, and a newspaper to be established at Maungākawa, near Cambridge, where Taingākawa was developing a Ngāti Hauā settlement.

Taingākawa's uncle Te Raihi Toroatai died in 1889, and his elder brother

Hote may also have died about this time, so that by the end of the 1880s events had begun to favour the emergence of Taingākawa as the effective leader of the King movement. He was literate in Māori, hard-working, forceful and fully committed to Māori self-government through the kingdom, which he regarded as legitimated by the Treaty of Waitangi and the Constitution Act 1852. His arguments were logical and eloquently stated.

Tāwhiao's Kauhanganui (Great Council) probably held its first session on 2 May 1889, a date that commemorated the anointing of the first King. Certainly from 1891, and probably from its inception, Taingākawa was the Speaker of the whare ariki (upper house). He was also described as the Tumuaki (leader) of the kingdom, a position similar to that of chief executive or prime minister. Working with T. T. Rāwhiti, the secretary of Te Kauhanganui, he organised the affairs of the kingdom through *Te Paki o Matariki*, the movement's newspaper. He announced the dates of parliamentary sessions, summarised debates and announced Te Kauhanganui's decisions. He set up the Tekau-mā-rua (the twelve), an executive council intended to free the King from the sole burden of carrying out the King movement programme. He set the agenda for Te Kauhanganui to debate; in 1893 it included such matters as decisions concerning the nature of the King movement government's seal, without which its laws would not be binding, and the rate of taxation. In August 1893 the decision was made to set up independent King movement land courts.

Tāwhiao died in August 1894. While his body lay in state at Taupiri, Taingākawa anointed Tāwhiao's son, Mahuta, as the third King and 'crowned' him with the Bible used by Tāmihana, who had placed a Bible over Pōtatau Te Wherowhero's head in 1859. The succession did not interrupt his reconstruction of the kingdom. A constitution was promulgated and a cabinet was announced with ministers responsible for various portfolios, and in the following years King movement magistrates, policemen, and a registrar for the kingdom's land court were appointed. Taingākawa announced that he was releasing the movement's followers from Tāwhiao's prohibition on schools: the King's government had decided to educate the movement's children. When Premier Richard Seddon visited Waikato in 1894, Taingākawa asked for a greater measure of Māori self-government and other concessions. When these were refused he continued his development of the kingdom regardless, unilaterally assuming powers to charge taxes, including dog taxes, and impose fines. From 1893 Europeans in the kingdom were warned that they too would have to obey the King's laws.

In May 1895 Te Keepa Te Rangihiwinui and Tūreiti Te Heuheu, in an attempt to unite the King movement with Te Kotahitanga (the movement for a Māori parliament to represent all tribes), brought Kotahitanga deeds of union to be signed at a Taupiri hui. Taingākawa quashed any tendency to unite the two movements, saying that Tāwhiao had left his own covenant, which would be signed in the Hauraki district and then circulated throughout New Zealand. In November 1897 Taingākawa visited Wellington at the invitation of the Kotahitanga chiefs. A meeting was arranged with Seddon to discuss the aspirations and grievances of Mahuta and his people. Taingākawa explained that they wished to live at peace under the authority of the Queen, but that their primary aim was to be empowered under the Treaty of Waitangi and the 1852 Constitution Act to administer their own affairs. He reminded Seddon of his petition, which outlined the evil effects of native land legislation on Māori, and asked him to support a bill being prepared by Hēnare Kaihau that would give effect to his concerns. In reply, Seddon outlined some of his still tentative plans for Māori land boards and limited self-government through councils. On 25 November Taingākawa appeared before the Native Affairs Committee with T. T. Rāwhiti and addressed the same issues.

Seddon's plans ultimately became the Native Lands Settlement and Administration Bill of 1898, the provisions of which failed to satisfy Taingākawa. He led a King movement delegation to Pāpāwai, Wairarapa, in 1898, and probably co-ordinated action with the Kotahitanga group opposed to the bill. Like them, he organised a petition, signed by himself and 5,975 others.

The beginnings of a split in the King movement arose from Mahuta's negotiations in 1898 with Seddon, his final acceptance of a seat on the Legislative Council in 1903, and his encouragement of the Waikato District Māori Land Council. Taingākawa was not given to this kind of compromise, and throughout the first three decades of the twentieth century relentlessly pursued the full King movement programme learnt in the 1860s from Tāwhiao. About 1906 he resurrected the idea of appealing to the British monarchy as Tāwhiao had done in 1884. He discussed the idea with Sir John Gorst, resident magistrate in the Waikato in the 1860s, who revisited New Zealand at this time. Gorst discouraged the idea, but by 1907 a petition to King Edward VII, drawn up by Taingākawa, was being circulated. At the same time he joined the Māori Rights Conservation Association, which championed equal rights for Māori and Europeans, and set up, with T. T. Rāwhiti and Hāmiora Mangakāhia, a federation of the Māori tribes of the North and South Islands which was a revived version of Te Kotahitanga.

The split with Mahuta was never total. The King attended the federation's first conference at Waahi, combined with the usual Kauhanganui session on 2 May. The discussion at this conference led to Taingākawa's major 1909 petition on the violation of land rights guaranteed by the Treaty of Waitangi. It was presented to the government for forwarding to England, and gave details of a number of specific grievances, including the Little Barrier Island purchase; it demanded full Māori autonomy.

The petition was ignored, but Taingākawa and his followers continued to collect signatures. At the 1910 rūnanganui (grand assembly) of the federation, Pēpene Eketone noted that 29,646 people had signed Taingākawa's petition. At this session a covenant confirmed Taingākawa as Tumuaki of the Māori kingdom, agreed to a ban on sales and leases he had imposed over the King movement lands, made him trustee of the lands, and agreed that his assent and seal were required to validate all the rules and laws adopted by the federation's committee. After some questioning, strong support by Hāmiora Mangakāhia ensured the covenant was adopted.

On 27 December 1911, as leader of Te Kotahitanga, Taingākawa symbolically signed a copy of the Treaty of Waitangi with Te Kahupūkoro of Ngāti Ruanui. This probably took place at the Christmas hui of the spiritual leader Mere Rikiriki, later the mentor of Tahupōtiki Wiremu Rātana. A year later she prophesied that the unity of the tribes under the

Treaty of Waitangi was blessed by God and would be guided by Te Kahupūkoro and Taingākawa.

Mahuta died on 9 November 1912. During the tangihanga a debate took place on the succession of Te Rata, Mahuta's son. James Carroll and others advised King movement leaders to abandon the title 'king'. But Taingākawa said it had been conferred by the Māori people on Pōtatau Te Wherowhero, whose successors had used it, and the title had been made tapu through the blood spilt in its defence. He declared his intention of crowning Te Rata king as he had Mahuta. This was done on 24 November 1912 beside Mahuta's casket.

Taingākawa declared in *Te Paki o Matariki* in January 1914 that his organisation, which he styled Te Kotahitanga Māori Motuhake, would act only under the authority of the King. By this time he was beginning to develop Rukumoana pa, near Morrinsville, as its new centre. He was proceeding with his plans to take his petition to England, and called on supporters to contribute £1 each. At a hui in April 1914, in spite of advice to the contrary from Āpirana Ngata, the decision was made to go. Te Rata, Taingākawa, Mita Karaka and Hōri T. Pāora (George G. Paul), the latter two acting as secretaries and interpreters, arrived in London on the *Niagara* in May 1914. They met with Sir John Gorst, but were disappointed in their hopes of assistance from him. On 4 June, dressed very correctly in frock coats, the group was received by King George V and Queen Mary. Compliments and gifts were exchanged, but no redress for grievances was forthcoming. A photograph taken on this occasion shows Taingākawa looking very distinguished, with grey hair and a dark moustache, the obvious leader of the group, seated beside a very young-looking Te Rata. The party sailed for New Zealand on the *Nestor* on 11 August 1914.

The First World War had commenced while they were still in London, and on their return Taingākawa and Te Rata were immediately embroiled in the issue of Māori military service. In 1915 Te Kauhanganui decided that no Waikato men should volunteer. By 1916 the King movement leadership was angered at what they saw as the persecution of the King's brothers. At a Waahi hui in November 1916, attended by the minister of defence, James Allen, Taingākawa declared that Waikato were reluctant for their young men to volunteer because their grievances dating from 1861 had not been addressed, and repeated the movement's official position that it was a matter for the young men concerned to decide. This prevented Te Rata or Taingākawa from being arrested for discouraging enlistment while making their position clear to their followers. The war ended without decisive measures being taken against the King movement's leaders, although police and defence reports made it clear that Taingākawa was among those regarded as responsible for Waikato intransigence.

As the influence of Te Puea Hērangi, Te Rata's cousin, and other younger King movement leaders increased, Taingākawa continued to build up Rukumoana as an alternative centre of power, establishing his parliament house there, building a church, and erecting a monument to King Mahuta. He also began to emphasise again the central importance of the Treaty of Waitangi. In 1919 he requested the prime minister, William Massey, to have it placed on record as an imperial document.

T. W. Rātana was, by now, becoming increasingly influential, and Taingākawa turned to him for help. His reliance on Rātana deepened the split with Te Puea. In 1920 Taingākawa led a delegation of King movement people to Rātana pa and appealed to Rātana to deal with Māori land grievances. Although he did not sign the Rātana covenant, he induced his own Ngāti Hauā and a significant faction of Waikato to support Rātana candidates in elections. In 1923 he presented a petition to the government asking for a commission of inquiry into the land confiscations of the 1860s. Like his 1909 petition, this laid great emphasis on Māori rights derived from the Treaty of Waitangi.

Taingākawa's petition was adopted and sponsored by Rātana from 25 May 1923 in the name of the United Māori Welfare League of the Northern, Southern and Chatham Islands. Taingākawa claimed that the petition and league were supported by 34,750 Māori, all desiring the unity of Māori under Jehovah. In 1924 Taingākawa and the prime minister of his Rukumoana parliament, Rēwiti Te Whena, joined Rātana's group travelling to London. They had two aims: to extend Rātana's ministry to England while raising funds for it, and to present Taingākawa's petition.

They hoped to persuade the League of Nations to intervene.

An attempt to get an interview with the secretary of state for the colonies failed, so the delegation arranged to be invited to a garden party at St James's Palace at which the prince of Wales was also a guest; he had met Taingākawa in New Zealand in 1920. The chiefs were presented to the prince, and gave him precious cloaks and an address. These were returned to the high commissioner, Sir James Allen, with a stiff note explaining that the prince could not receive gifts unless forwarded through the proper channels and recommended by the New Zealand government. Protests were made at the insult of returned gifts and the petition was sent to the Colonial Office, but the group was able to achieve little more in England.

In New Zealand in later years, Taingākawa's petition was often credited with having helped bring about the royal commission of 1927, which investigated the confiscations, acknowledged some government faults, and recommended monetary compensation for them. Taingākawa also influenced Rātana into making ratification of the Treaty of Waitangi by the New Zealand government a central plank of his party's policy in the 1920s and early 1930s.

Tupu Atanatiu Taingākawa Te Waharoa died on 24 June 1929 in Awanui Private Hospital, Auckland, aged 84. His wife, Rakapa, had predeceased him, but he was survived by a son, Tarapīpipi, who became the third kingmaker and crowned Korokī in 1933. At Tupu Taingākawa's death Rukumoana was falling into decay, and Te Puea's faction had moved the kingdom on to new paths. Ngata told Peter Buck that a new generation of leaders knew little of Taingākawa. Yet his work ensured the survival and the continuity of the kingdom and forced officialdom to show wary respect for the successive Māori Kings. His insistence on ratification of the Treaty of Waitangi and his demands for the redress of grievances foreshadowed events of the late twentieth century.

Angela Ballara

Love, R. H. N. 'Policies of frustration: the growth of Māori politics; the Rātana/Labour era'.
    PhD thesis, Victoria University of Wellington, 1977
Williams, J. A. *Politics of the New Zealand Māori*. Seattle, 1969
Worger, W. H. 'Te Puea, the Kīngitanga, and Waikato'. MA thesis, University of Auckland, 1974

T. T. Rāwhiti
fl. 1887–1922

Ngāti Hauā; King movement secretary and administrator

T. T. Rāwhiti was closely associated, for some 30 years, with demands for Māori autonomy and self-sufficiency. He probably came from Tauwhare, near Cambridge, and had affiliations with Ngāti Hauā. The names of his parents are not known, and his own personal names are not recorded: he preferred to be known simply as T. T. Rāwhiti, occasionally referred to as P. T. T. Rāwhiti or T. T. Rāwhiti Maaka, and is probably the Maaka Rāwhiti whose name is recorded in electoral rolls in 1908 and 1919.

Rāwhiti may have been a native agent in the King Country in the late 1880s; he appears in the court records in 1887. He became a close associate of Tupu Taingākawa, Speaker of the upper house of Te Kauhanganui (the King movement's parliament); Rāwhiti was its secretary. The published list of laws passed at the 1892 and 1893 sessions of Te Kauhanganui appeared over his name and he was the author of many of the published reports on its proceedings.

Rāwhiti played a prominent role in many of the activities of the King movement between 1892 and 1922, although his alliance with Taingākawa put him out of favour with the movement's leaders from time to time. Rāwhiti played a major role in Te Peeke o Aotearoa, the bank established by King Tāwhiao in 1886; he was probably its organiser and manager. He signed the only two cheques known to have been issued on the bank, in 1894, although his involvement may well have lasted longer than that: the bank operated from 1886 until about 1905.

In June 1895 Rāwhiti served on a joint committee of Te Kotahitanga and King movement representatives, which apparently considered a suggestion for the union of the two movements. In the same year he vigorously defended the King movement's right to impose its own dog taxes. He visited Wellington with Tupu Taingākawa in November 1897. They asked Premier Richard Seddon to support a bill prepared by Hēnare Kaihau, MHR for Western Māori, which would let Māori administer their own affairs. They made the same plea before the Native Affairs Committee of Parliament. In June 1898 Rāwhiti was a leading member of the delegation sent by the Māori King, Mahuta, to the Kotahitanga parliament at Pāpāwai. Here he was elected to a committee that decided on the wording of an amendment to the Native Lands Settlement and Administration Bill, then before Parliament. He later gave evidence at the committee hearings on the bill.

By 1900 Rāwhiti was acting as private secretary to King Mahuta; at a hui at Waahi, near Huntly, he stated Māori objections to the Māori Lands Administration Act 1900. He represented Waikato at the New Zealand International Exhibition in Christchurch in 1906. In 1907 he was prominent in the revival of Te Kotahitanga, which included a petition to King Edward VII to treat Māori and European equally in terms of the Treaty of Waitangi. He attended a meeting of 3,000 people at Waahi in May 1907 to discuss treaty issues, and described its aim as being to present a united Māori front to the government. He wanted Māori to have the power to manage their own affairs according to their own customs, although the Māori government would act in harmony with the general government.

In 1909 a government delegation met with Mahuta and his supporters at Waahi. The ensuing conference agreed to allocate land in the King Country for Pākehā settlement, and to provide reserves, land for Māori farms and land for Mahuta. James Cowan wrote of 'Big Te Rāwhiti, the suave and smiling secretary' of the King movement, playing a prominent role at this hui. Taingākawa and Rāwhiti disagreed with Mahuta's acceptance of the government's terms. At a hui in April 1910 at Waharoa, north of Matamata, they announced the formation of a federation of the Māori tribes of New Zealand, under the Treaty of Waitangi. Nevertheless, Rāwhiti's involvement in Te Kauhanganui continued, as secretary, treasurer and a participant in debates; he was also involved in other tribal meetings.

Rāwhiti continued his involvement with Taingākawa's organisation during and after the First World War, continuing to act as treasurer until at least 1920. He was still active in King movement affairs in 1922, when he spoke at a hui at Waahi, and he played a crucial role during the visit of T. W. Rātana to King Te Rata, Mahuta's successor, in October 1922. That is the last recorded reference to him. His date of death is not known.

Stuart Park

Cowan, J. *The Maoris of New Zealand.* Christchurch, 1910

Park, G. S. 'Te Peeke o Aotearoa: the bank of King Tāwhiao'. *New Zealand Journal of History* 26, No 2 (Oct. 1992): 161–183

Te huihuinga ki Waharoa, Aperira 7, 1910. Hamilton, 1910

Part Four

Te Rata

Tonga Mahuta

Te Puea Hērangi

Piupiu Te Wherowhero

The delegation to London in 1914: Te Rata (standing, left) with Mita Karaka and Hōri T. Pāora; Tupu Taingākawa Te Waharoa seated in front.

Te Rata

1877-80?–1933

Tainui and Ngāti Mahuta leader, fourth Māori King

Te Rata Mahuta was the fourth leader of the Māori King movement. He inherited many of the qualities and advantages which conferred leadership on his predecessors, with the added support of 50 years of widespread Māori recognition of the special status conferred by his role as king.

Te Rata was born sometime between 1877 and 1880 at his father's home, Hukanui, near Waahi pa, Huntly. He was the eldest of five sons of the third Māori King, Mahuta Tāwhiao Pōtatau Te Wherowhero of Ngāti Mahuta. Te Rata's mother was Te Marae, a daughter of Amukete (Amuketi) Te Kerei, a chief killed at the battle at Rangiriri in November 1863. Te Rata is said to have been well educated, but was a chronic invalid as a child, and in adulthood suffered from rheumatoid arthritis and heart disease. Partly because of his physical disabilities his contemporaries tended to regard him as weak, shy and easily led, and attributed his role in many important events to the influence of other King movement leaders. Te Rata usually lived quietly at Waahi, although he sometimes attended race meetings in Auckland. He married Te Uranga, the daughter of Iriwhata Wharemaki and Hira Wati of Ngāti Korokī; their two sons were Korokī and Taipū.

Te Rata's life was punctuated with controversy. From 1908 Hēnare Kaihau set up land agencies in Auckland with the aim of raising money to buy back confiscated lands. Te Rata invested heavily in these. By 1911 it was becoming apparent that the investments were losing money and both Te Rata and his father were becoming disillusioned with their agent. That year Te Rata represented Mahuta at an important hui at Parewanui near Bulls to select a candidate for the Western Māori parliamentary seat. This had been held by Kaihau, but leaders from Taranaki were anxious to appoint a younger, better educated man who could help them gain compensation for confiscated lands. Because of the obligations of their position, and because Kaihau was still their agent in selling and leasing their land, Mahuta and Te Rata could not lightly shift their allegiance from him. Te Rata did not openly support the aims of the Taranaki elders, but he demonstrated his considerable talent for diplomacy by asking whether they had a suitable candidate who could renew the ties between Waikato and Taranaki. In this way he cleared the way for the selection of Māui Pōmare, the candidate preferred by his father. Although he was later opposed by Te Puea Hērangi and others, Te Rata continued to support Pōmare as MP, both out of respect for his father's wishes and because Pōmare promised to set up a commission of inquiry into the Waikato confiscations.

Mahuta died on 9 November 1912 at Waahi. There was no doubt that Te Rata was the most suitable candidate to succeed his father, and it was thought that his knowledge of Pākehā affairs would help his people. Some Māori leaders advised Te Rata to abandon the title of king, substituting the Māori supreme title, ariki. Tupu Taingākawa Te Waharoa, the King movement's premier, successfully opposed this, stressing the continuity of the kingship and the fact that Pōtatau, the first Māori King, had been made king by the Māori people. On 24 November 1912 he invested Te Rata with the kingship beside his father's body. Te Rata then assumed the name Pōtatau Te Wherowhero.

Te Rata was thought to have inherited his father's personal property, estimated to be worth £20,000, and land to the value of £100,000. It is likely, though, that his financial position was much less satisfactory. Apart from the failure of Kaihau's investments, family members including his cousin, Hera Hērangi, and Mahuta had been selling land on their own account for years. In addition, Mahuta's property had been divided among his sons.

In 1913 Te Rata took up Tupu Taingākawa's plans to present the British

Crown with yet another petition asking for the restoration of confiscated lands. His mother, Te Marae, sold family land to finance the expedition, and King movement members agreed to support the trip by contributing a shilling each. A hui was held at Waahi on 1 April 1914 at which several speakers, including Āpirana Ngata, attempted to convince Te Rata and Taingākawa to cancel their expedition. But they departed on 11 April, with Mita Karaka and Hōri Tiro Pāora as secretaries and interpreters, arriving in London in late May.

Te Rata had counted on the assistance of Sir John Gorst, government agent in Waikato in the 1860s and now resident in England; he at first refused to see the delegation, and gave them no real support. They were eventually received by King George V and Queen Mary, but the British government reiterated its position that Māori must look to the New Zealand government for the redress of grievances. The expedition, during which Te Rata fell ill, was a failure, but his reception by the British royal family (he was the first Māori King to meet a reigning British monarch) confirmed his pre-eminent status, recognised by Waikato and King Country Māori and Pākehā. He was welcomed back at a hui organised by Te Puea at Te Paina marae, Mercer, and given a reception and ball by the mayor and citizens of the town.

Te Rata was adroit at evading confrontation damaging to his mana. The First World War had commenced while he was still in England, and on his return he was asked whether Māori should assist the British King by enlisting. He is reported to have recommended diplomatically that the matter be left to individual choice: with other King movement leaders he felt that the confiscation issue needed resolution before Waikato men could be encouraged to enlist. Also, the King movement had revived and adopted the Pai Mārire religion, whose adherents were opposed to military service.

In 1915 Te Rata was criticised for his failure to encourage Waikato volunteers. Later he undertook to protect a Māori recruit who deserted and came to his house at Waahi. This action provoked a request from a senior army officer for his prosecution, but the action did not proceed. When James Allen, minister of defence, visited Waikato in 1916, Te Rata absented himself from the meeting, nominating Tupu Taingākawa as his representative. Taingākawa repeated Te Rata's opinion that the decision to volunteer was a matter for the young men concerned. Te Rata's younger brother Tonga was repeatedly prosecuted for failing to report for territorial duty; and the youngest brother, Te Rauangaanga, was taken forcibly for training at Narrow Neck, Auckland, in July 1918.

In March 1919 a new building for Te Rata's parliament was opened in Ngāruawāhia; he was too ill to attend. In April 1920 Te Rata, through Pōmare, asked the government for the opportunity to show Waikato's loyalty to the Crown by welcoming the visiting prince of Wales in the new house. Incensed at his attitude to conscription, and as a discouragement to the King movement, the government denied his request. Te Rata went ahead with preparations, and on 27 April he stood on Ngāruawāhia station with his supporters, but the prince's train passed through without stopping. Offended by this humiliation, Waikato remained aloof from the Māori welcome at Rotorua.

Plans to re-establish the centre of the King movement at Ngāruawāhia, according to the wish of Te Rata's grandfather, Tāwhiao, continued. Te Rata's adviser, John Ormsby, purchased for him a 10-acre site on the east bank of the Waikato River. Tūrangawaewae was to be a marae for his tribe, and also for all those who acknowledged his authority and that of his successors.

From 1922 Te Rata was subject to pressure from all sides on the subject of the new Rātana faith. His cousin, Piupiu Te Wherowhero, was strongly Rātana, as were many of his Tekau-mā-rua (council of 12), and they made frequent attempts to draw him in. Te Puea was as strongly opposed to Rātana affiliation. Te Rata, committed to supporting Pōmare as his best hope for the redress of Waikato's grievances, refused to sign Rātana's covenant.

A breach developed between the two movements over the issue of the parliamentary candidate for Western Māori. A meeting at Ngāruawāhia in September 1922 between T. W. Rātana and Te Rata was intended to heal the breach; Rātana and 300 followers arrived, but what was seen as a slight to the King's mana prevented the meeting from taking place. A hui in March

1929 for the opening of the Māhinārangi meeting house at Tūranga-waewae marae was attended by Rātana and a large group of followers. This resulted in more friendly relations but little increased co-operation between the two movements. On subsequent visits, there were times when Te Rata crept out of his house, disguised, to avoid meeting Rātana. In 1930, on the death of Pōmare, Te Rata successfully supported Te Tāite Te Tomo as the Western Māori candidate against Rātana.

In 1928 Te Puea was instrumental in arranging a visit by the governor general, Sir Charles Fergusson, to Ngāruawāhia. However, the King movement leadership were still resentful of the government's conscription tactics against members of Te Rata's family and people, and at its failure to restore the confiscated lands (the royal commission eventually obtained by Pōmare offered compensation in the same year). Te Rata refused to meet Fergusson when he visited Tūrangawaewae on 30 April.

In the 1920s, as his illness progressed and formerly trusted advisers such as Tupu Taingākawa turned to Rātana, Te Rata abandoned his parliament, known as Te Kauhanganui, as an instrument of his policy making and leaned more on Te Puea, who became his mouthpiece to an increasing extent. Āpirana Ngata's schemes to develop Māori land through government loan money, initiated in November 1929, were enthusi-astically accepted by Te Puea, but many Waikato people resisted involve-ment because of lingering suspicion of the government. Ngata and Te Raumoa Balneavis discussed land development with Te Rata at the opening of Māhinārangi in 1929, and subsequently the King came to accept their ideas. In 1931 and 1932 Te Rata and his brothers gave Te Puea their support on land development. Te Rata's sanction of the schemes ensured their success and he successfully persuaded many formerly suspicious landowners to allow their blocks to be developed. With his brothers he developed 600 acres on his own account. Ngata was later to say that Te Rata's death removed a great influence for progress; had he lived he would have been the greatest champion of land settlement.

Te Rata had been ill more or less continuously from 1927. In the last three years of his life he suffered from acute rheumatism. He died at Waahi on 1 October 1933. Te Uranga died in December 1935. Their younger son, Taipū, had died while at school; the elder son, Korokī, only in his mid 20s at Te Rata's death, succeeded him. Te Rata's tangihanga lasted a week. Te Puea was in charge of the arrangements; the thousands of mourners were accommodated in marquees, and hundreds of sheep and cattle were slaughtered to feed them. Rātana arrived on 8 October, and at last paid his respects to Te Rata face to face.

Te Rata was buried on Taupiri Mountain on 8 October; the funeral procession included Ngata, J. G. Coates, and H. E. Holland. The weather had been fine throughout the tangihanga, but as the coffin was borne up Taupiri rain fell heavily in a sign of mourning from the land itself.

Angela Ballara

Jones, P. Te H. 'Māori Kings'. In *The Māori people in the nineteen-sixties.* Ed. E. Schwimmer. Auckland, 1968

King, M. *Te Puea.* Auckland, 1977

Love, R. H. N. 'Policies of frustration: the growth of Māori politics; the Rātana/Labour era'. PhD thesis, Victoria University of Wellington, 1977

Mahuta, R. 'The Māori King movement today'. In *Tihe mauri ora.* Ed. M. King. [Wellington], 1978

Tonga Mahuta
1892/93?–1947

Ngāti Mahuta leader

Tonga Mahuta was born probably in 1892 or 1893 at his father's home at Hukanui, near Waahi pā, Huntly. He was the fourth surviving son of Mahuta Tāwhiao Pōtatau Te Wherowhero, the third Māori King. His mother was Te Marae, a daughter of the chief Amukete (Amuketi) Te Kerei, who had been killed during the fighting at Rangiriri in November 1863. Tonga's eldest brother was the fourth King, Te Rata. His main tribal affiliation was with Ngāti Mahuta, but the family was connected by senior lines of descent to many major tribal groups. Little or nothing is remembered of Tonga's upbringing or education. During his childhood there were few native schools in the Waikato–King Country area, and it is probable that he was privately taught.

In 1914, when the First World War commenced, Tonga was in his early 20s. The leaders of the King movement were reluctant to allow their young men to volunteer for service in the New Zealand Expeditionary Force because the issue of the confiscation of Waikato lands had not been resolved, and because they held to the revived Tariao form of the Pai Mārire religion. Tonga Mahuta refused to report for territorial training in 1914 and was fined. In early 1916 he was prosecuted again with a few others from Waahi, selected from among leading families in the hope that the example would break resistance. He was fined five shillings. In April 1916 he was prosecuted again. On 26 June 1916 Major E. H. Northcroft visited Waahi. The King movement leaders there reproved him; they were concerned that Tonga, a member of the Māori royal family, was being pressured about territorial training when they saw Europeans of similar status exempt. Tonga was prosecuted again in April 1917.

In June 1917 a proclamation extending the provisions of the Military Service Act 1916 rendered Māori liable to be called up for military service to the Native Expeditionary Force Reserve. The minister of defence, James Allen, reassured Te Arawa petitioners and other 'loyal' tribes that the measure would be used only against Waikato.

Tonga Mahuta was called up in the ballot of 25 June 1918; his name had been confirmed through use of confidential census information. On 7 June three constables had gone to Te Paina, Mercer, where the King movement people were debating conscription, and arrested seven Māori, including Tonga's younger brother Te Rauangaanga. He was taken to Narrow Neck camp, Auckland, where Māui Pōmare, his member of Parliament, and Colonel G. W. S. Patterson were able to persuade him to take the oath of allegiance and to write a letter, later distributed among Waikato Māori, saying that it was better to go into camp and not to flout the law. Probably because of his brother's letter, when Tonga was arrested on 24 August he called out to the 44 taken with him to accompany him to camp, without resistance.

Thirty-four Waikato Māori arrested with Tonga consistently refused to wear military uniform or to train, and were punished with 'dietary deprivation' (bread and water) and various periods of imprisonment. Six were court-martialled and sentenced to two years in gaol with hard labour. It was believed by the military authorities that Tonga's cousin Te Puea Hērangi had Prussian ancestry through her grandfather, William Searancke, and that Waikato Māori were German sympathisers. Perhaps to dispel this notion, and out of support for Te Rauangaanga, by September Tonga had consented to wear uniform and to train. Not long afterwards the war came to an end, and by June 1919 all trainees at Narrow Neck and all prisoners were released. Outstanding warrants for arrests of Māori were not executed.

Tonga Mahuta married Te Okewhare, the daughter of Te Awaiti Hiko and Te Aira Hiko, both of Ngāti Naho. There were at least three sons and three daughters of the marriage. Tonga was interested in rugby league as a young man, and was later made a life member of the New Zealand Rugby

Football League. His interest in sport continued, and by 1925 he was a member of the Māori Advisory Board of the New Zealand Rugby Football Union.

King Te Rata was often either ill or unwilling to meet official visitors, and his brothers, including Tonga, deputised for him. During the struggles that raged among leaders of the King movement over the Rātana movement, Tonga and his brothers gradually came to support Te Rata and Te Puea rather than the Rātana faction led by Piupiu Te Wherowhero and Tupu Taingākawa. They also came to accept the plans of Āpirana Ngata concerning land consolidation. By 1929 Ngata considered that Tonga Mahuta was a progressive leader who would teach Waikato what was possible in the way of land management. In February and March 1932 Tonga accompanied Te Rata to Kāwhia to encourage land consolidation schemes, and organised the development of 600 acres for Te Rata and his other brothers. After Te Rata's death in 1933, Tonga and his brothers competed with Te Puea for influence over the young fifth King, Korokī.

During the Second World War, Tonga Mahuta was more supportive of the war effort than some Waikato people would have liked. Te Puea and other King movement leaders permitted individual young Waikato men to enlist if they chose, but the confiscation issue was still not settled: the compensation offered in 1928 had been refused, and Waikato felt that their young men had little reason to be loyal to the government. They were willing to allow their men to defend New Zealand itself, and to assist with the growing of extra food, but little more. Tonga Mahuta supported this line, but took it a little further, actively encouraging Waikato Māori to join the Home Guard. After a meeting in Wellington in which Te Puea and other leaders discussed with Prime Minister Peter Fraser the Waikato attitude to the war effort, Tonga organised the voluntary transfer of Waikato people into industries such as the coalmines and freezing works. He encouraged his people to raise essential foodstuffs and to contribute to patriotic funds. For a period he was associated with the National Service Department in Hamilton.

The confiscation issue was temporarily laid to rest in 1946 with the acceptance by Te Puea and other King movement leaders of a monetary settlement. The Tainui Māori Trust Board was set up to administer the annual payments. When the first funds arrived Tonga suggested that each year the money should be used to purchase a farm for each of the many hapū affected by the confiscation. His suggestion was not carried out. Tonga Mahuta died of tuberculosis at Waahi pā, on 13 March 1947. His body was taken from Waahi to Tūrangawaewae for a huge tangihanga, and he was buried on Taupiri Mountain. Te Okewhare had died on 13 March 1944, and Tonga was survived by six children.

All his life Tonga Mahuta had lived at Waahi in the home formerly occupied by his father, King Mahuta. He had been one of a group of Waahi leaders who, while recognising Te Puea's role as one leader of the King movement, resisted her efforts to monopolise authority. He had assisted the King movement to maintain its separate identity and to continue its development as a major force in the Māori world.

Angela Ballara

King, M. *Te Puea*. Auckland, 1977
Mahuta, R. 'The Māori King movement today'. In *Tihe mauri ora*. Ed. M. King. [Wellington], 1978
Obit. *Evening Post*. 14 March 1947: 9

Te Puea Hērangi
1883–1952

Waikato woman of mana, Kīngitanga leader

Te Puea Hērangi was born at Whatiwhatihoe, near Pirongia, on 9 November 1883. Her mother was Tiahuia, daughter of Tāwhiao Te Wherowhero of Ngāti Mahuta, the second Māori King, and his senior wife, Hera. Her father was Te Tahuna Hērangi, son of William Searancke, an English surveyor, and Hāriata Rangitaupa of Ngāti Ngāwaero hapu of Ngāti Maniapoto. Te Puea was thus born into the kāhui ariki, the family of the first Māori King, Pōtatau Te Wherowhero, in the difficult years following the wars of the 1860s and the extensive confiscation of Tainui lands. She was to play a crucial role alongside three successive kings in re-establishing the Kīngitanga as a central force among the Tainui people, and in achieving national recognition of its importance.

Te Puea's family moved when she was young to Pukekawa and then to Mangatāwhiri, near Mercer, and between 1895 and 1898 she attended primary schools in Mercer and Auckland. She was known to her family as Te Kirihaehae. Her young adult years were exuberant, and she had several short-lived relationships. During one in particular – with a Pākehā, Roy Seccombe – she cut herself off from her people. Mahuta, Te Puea's uncle and successor to Tāwhiao as king, himself intervened in about 1910 to draw her back. He had picked her out in her childhood as having unusual abilities, and had spent many hours passing on his knowledge to her; now he appealed to her to remember her duty to the Kīngitanga and the people. Te Puea returned to Mangatāwhiri and took up a burden that sat heavily upon her.

The early years in particular were difficult, because there was some resentment of her new position (her main support came from the people of Mercer and the lower Waikato); but she persevered with courage against the odds. She had her first test as a leader in 1911. Mahuta had decided to approve Māui Pōmare as parliamentary candidate for Western Māori in place of Hēnare Kaihau, previously the nominee of the Kīngi-tanga. Te Puea accompanied Pōmare around the villages of the lower Waikato; her support ensured his election.

Te Puea's influence became more firmly established among Tainui people during the First World War, when she led their opposition to the government's conscription policy. She understood the sense of alienation that the military invasion, occupation and confiscation of land had im-posed upon the people, and understood, too, that the Kīngitanga held the key to restoring their sense of purpose. Te Puea was guided all her life by Tāwhiao's sayings; more than anyone else, she gathered them together. During the war she drew on Tāwhiao's words forbidding Waikato to take up arms again after he had finally made his peace with the Crown in 1881. She stood firm with those men who did not wish to fight a war that was not theirs, on behalf of a government that had dispossessed and scattered their people. But the government was impatient with what it saw as defiance and disloyalty, and compounded Tainui feelings of injustice by conscripting Māori only from the Waikato–Maniapoto district.

At this difficult time Te Puea's leadership was of great importance to Tainui. The revival of the Pai Mārire faith, brought to Waikato from Taranaki by Tāwhiao, helped to strengthen the people. Te Puea expressed her own opposition to conscription in specially composed waiata such as 'E huri rā koe', 'Kāti nei e te iwi te kumekume roa' and 'Ngā rā o Hune ka ara te pakanga', and gathered together the men liable for conscription at Te Paina (the pā she had rebuilt at Mangatāwhiri) to support them. They were balloted in groups in 1918, then arrested and taken to Narrow Neck training camp at Auckland, where they were subjected to severe military punishments if they refused to wear uniform. Te Puea would travel north and sit outside where the men could see her from time to time; it gave them much-needed encouragement.

Te Puea was now determined to rebuild a centre for the Kīngitanga at

TŪRONGO HOUSE, NGĀRUAWĀHIA

Te Puea with other children. From left, standing: Tuhi Hira and Te Ranga Poutapu; seated: Wanikore Hērangi, Te Puea, Te Atarua Hērangi, Tāmati Hērangi.

Ngāruawāhia, its original home before the confiscation, in accordance with Tāwhiao's wishes. She was dissatisfied with the swampy conditions at Mangatāwhiri and wished to make a new start in the wake of the tragic influenza epidemic of late 1918, which had struck the settlement with devastating effect, leaving a quarter of the people dead. Te Puea gathered up 100 orphaned children from lower Waikato and placed them in the care of the remaining families. But she needed a better home for them. In 1920 Waikato leaders were able to buy 10 acres of confiscated land on the bank of the Waikato River opposite the township and by 1921 Te Puea was ready to begin moving the people from Mangatāwhiri to build a new marae, to be called Tūrangawaewae. It seemed an impossible plan, given the distance the people had to travel and their lack of resources, and Te Puea was frank with them about the difficulties they would face. Years of hard work followed, draining and filling swampy scrub-covered land, and raising funds for the building of a sleeping house for visitors and, later, a large carved house intended as a hospital. They had also to overcome the attitudes of the Pākehā citizens of Ngāruawāhia, who initially tried to have them removed from the borough.

In these years a community was welded together under Te Puea's leadership. In the evenings an expert in haka taught the young people, and Te Puea formed a group named Te Pou o Mangatāwhiri. Its name commemorates the pou (post) erected by the Kīngitanga at Mangatāwhiri beyond which Pākehā were not to acquire land or authority, an injunction they ignored. Te Pou o Mangatāwhiri set out to raise the hundreds of pounds needed for the carved house by performing in halls and theatres throughout the North Island. Te Puea kept morale high on the tours, gathering the young people together to tell them stories and share her hopes with them, joking, jumping to her feet to show them how to improve their haka, how to pūkana. In 1927 they toured the East Coast, where Āpirana Ngata, MP for Eastern Māori, led Ngāti Porou in giving strong support to the building of the carved house. It was the start of a long friendship between Te Puea and Ngata. At his suggestion the house was named Māhinārangi, after the ancestor who had united Tainui with the tribes of the East Coast. Six thousand people attended the hui to open the house in March 1929.

Other events of significance to the Kīngitanga occurred in the 1920s. In 1927 a royal commission chaired by W. A. Sim considered the confiscation of land in the 1860s. It recommended the payment of £3,000 annually to Waikato as compensation; both the offer and some of the commission's findings were unacceptable, and negotiations over a settlement occupied the next 20 years. Te Puea was also increasingly becoming known outside Waikato. Her friendship with Ngata and Gordon Coates led her into frequent contacts with government officials, and another friend, Eric Ramsden, a journalist, persuaded her of the value of publicity for her work. Articles about 'Princess' Te Puea began to appear in newspapers and magazines.

With Tūrangawaewae marae established, Te Puea turned her attention to building an economic base for the people, dependent until now on seasonal wage-labour, and already feeling the impact of the depression. Ngata became native minister at the end of 1928, and his legislation providing for state loans to Māori farmers put land development within the reach of Waikato. The development schemes began on small pockets of land at Waiuku and Onewhero. Te Puea became the supervisor of the schemes and travelled constantly among them, taking families from Ngāruawāhia to help with the work. She shared Ngata's vision of land development and dairy farming as the basis of strong communities; and as the farms were subdivided and homes and milking sheds built, she established or extended marae throughout Waikato. Sometimes she chose the place herself, as at Mangatangi and Rākaumanga, supervising all the arrangements from cutting the trees to plastering the walls with cement over soaked, cleaned sacks. At Mangatangi she named the house Tamaoho, and had a great canvas painted telling the story of Tamaoho, and the migration of Ngāti Tamaoho long before from Maungakiekie (One Tree Hill) through the Hūnua Range into the Mangatangi area. The dining hall here is named for her: Kirihaehae. New marae were incorporated into the round of Poukai gatherings instituted by Tāwhiao, which are still at the heart of the Kīngitanga: an annual visit by the King – and, more recently, the Queen – to each marae to consult the people.

By the mid 1930s the Tūrangawaewae community was well established. In 1940 Te Puea was able to buy a farm close to the marae, which she hoped would bring in an income to sustain Tūrangawaewae. She and her husband Rāwiri Tūmōkai Kātipa (whom she had married at the wish of the kāhui ariki in 1922) lived there for the next 12 years, and a whole generation grew up working on the farm. Te Puea left the Kīngitanga strong because of the central beliefs with which the young people grew to adulthood: faith, dedication to the Kīngitanga, respect for kawa, the importance of caring for visitors, and the value of hard work. Each day began and ended with Pai Mārire karakia, drawing the people together from wherever they were working. This day-to-day expression of unity was of great importance to Te Puea; it reflected long-held Kīngitanga beliefs that the burden of the wars and the confiscation must be carried by the people together if they were to find the strength to survive it. So Te Puea never mentioned hapū (though she was an acknowledged expert on whakapapa); nor did she encourage the people to identify themselves by hapū. They thought of themselves as Waikato.

By the late 1930s Te Puea and the Kīngitanga had attracted increasing official recognition. She was appointed a CBE in 1937. The following year, the governor general, Lord Galway, officially opened Tūrongo, the striking carved house that Te Puea had built for King Korokī at Tūrangawaewae; it was named for the ancestor who had married Māhinārangi. Because of the improvement in Kīngitanga relations with the government, Te Puea was willing to contemplate Waikato's joining the Waitangi centennial celebrations in 1940. Some years before she had set out to restore the skill of canoe building. Rānui Maupakanga supervised the refitting of the old canoe, Te Winika, by a team of younger carvers. Te Puea's vision of a fleet representing the traditional voyaging canoes came closer to fulfilment. In 1936 the government seemed willing to help a project that could also serve a purpose at the Waitangi centennial; but the funds were slow in coming, and eventually only one canoe, Ngā-toki-mata-whao-rua, was completed in time.

Tainui ultimately stayed away from Waitangi in 1940. Te Puea was affronted by the government's refusal to exempt Korokī from the necessity to register under the Social Security Act of 1938, seeing this as evidence of its continuing failure to recognise his mana. But she was also angered by the fate of an action brought by Hoani Te Heuheu Tūkino, of Ngāti Tūwharetoa, against the Aotea District Māori Land Board to prevent Māori land being charged for the payment of debts. Late in 1938 the case went to the Court of Appeal, which would not countenance Ngāti Tūwharetoa attempts to rely on the Treaty of Waitangi because it was not part of domestic law. The Tainui boycott of the Waitangi celebrations made the headlines, and Te Puea was reported to have quoted with approval the saying of an elder: 'This is an occasion for rejoicing on the part of the pakehas and those tribes who have not suffered any injustices during the past 100 years.'

Te Puea had been raised with a 'bitter, poignant memory' of the 1860s war and confiscations. As a child she had heard stories first hand from those who had suffered in the fighting. But she was very anxious for a settlement so that the people could begin to put the pain of the past behind them. In 1946 she decided to accept Prime Minister Peter Fraser's

Te Puea Hērangi.

offer of £5,000 per year in perpetuity, to be administered by the Tainui
Māori Trust Board, not because it was an adequate settlement of the
people's losses, but because she was immensely practical, and knew it was
the best deal she could get at the time. Above all, it was a vindication.

Te Puea's depth of feeling about the confiscation, however, never
affected her many personal friendships with Pākehā – some of them very
close – nor her strong belief that the two peoples should learn to respect
one another's cultures so that they could live comfortably together. She
sometimes talked intensely about this, tracing along two fingers the
parallel paths of two canoes – Māori and Pākehā. Māori, she said, should
show the Pākehā what was good in Māori culture, and should in turn take
from Pākehā friends what was good in theirs. In informal conversation she
tried to convey to Pākehā politicians an understanding of central Māori
values. When Peter Fraser asked her opinion about a current concern of
employers that Māori were unreliable because they tended to disappear to
tangihanga, Te Puea tried to explain: Māori had to live and work in a
Pākehā world, but a Māori attending a tangihanga or a hui 'comes back
right into the middle of things Māori ... he recharges his Māori batteries.'

One of the measures of Te Puea's achievements is that she achieved a
national status for the Kīngitanga among both Māori and Pākehā.
Mahuta had tried to bridge the gap between Tainui and the Crown by
going to Wellington as a member of the Legislative Council; Te Puea
bridged it by inviting governors general and politicians – Reform, United,
and Labour in succession – to Ngāruawāhia. If distinguished visitors
came to honour the Kīngitanga it would help the people to overcome
their suspicion of government.

Yet friendship with the government never meant compromise when
Māori rights were at stake. In 1931 she secured the dismissal of a Pākehā
supervisor of the Waiuku land development schemes, Patrick Barry, because she thought him preoccupied with cost-cutting and lacking in
sympathy with the broader purpose of the schemes. During the Second
World War she still would not encourage Tainui men to enlist, though she
raised thousands of pounds for the Red Cross. In 1941 she told Fraser,
'Look, Peter, it's perfectly simple. I'm not anti-Pākehā; I'm not pro-

German; I'm pro-Māori.' And in 1940 she supported Ngāti Whātua against the government and the Auckland City Council, who were trying to evict the people from their remaining fragments of ancestral land at Ōkahu Bay. Her friendship with Fraser was strained by her active involvement.

Throughout her life Te Puea strengthened Kīngitanga networks beyond Tainui. She travelled a great deal, often (in later years) with King Korokī, and through personal friendships established lasting relationships among many tribes in Taranaki, the Whanganui district, on the East Coast, and in the far north. This in turn helped the re-establishment of people's belief in the importance of the Kīngitanga and in the Waikato people as its guardian. Te Puea's close friendship with Tau Hēnare of Ngāti Hine, MP for Northern Māori, is reflected in the inscription of her words in the meeting house at Mōtatau, far from home: 'Ka mahi au, ka inoi au, ka moe au, ka mahi anō' (I work, I pray, I sleep, and then I work again). This was the answer Te Puea had given the Pākehā press when they wanted to know what to write about her when she received her CBE. Her vision of the unity of the tribes was obvious in her enthusiasm for the celebrations in 1950 for the 600th anniversary of the arrival of the 'Great Fleet' of traditional voyaging canoes, conceived by Ngata and Peter Buck as a series of national hui. Te Puea joined with Ngata in planning the hui, and she had nine model canoes carved for the final hui at Tūrangawaewae, to be presented to descendants of the chiefs of the first canoes. Beyond New Zealand, she established relationships in the Pacific, travelling in 1947 to Tonga and the Cook Islands. With her she took King Korokī's daughter, Piki, the future Māori Queen Te Ātairangikaahu. Te Puea was conscious of past links with other Polynesian peoples, and hoped that this visit would make possible future contact with them. She also saw the importance for the Kīngitanga of strengthening a sense of identity with other hereditary Polynesian leaderships.

In other ways, too, Te Puea looked to the future of the people. She changed her mind about the dangers of Pākehā education, becoming a member of a school committee. Korokī wanted his adopted son, Robert Te Kotahi Mahuta, to be a mechanic, but Te Puea intervened to send him instead to Mount Albert Grammar School in Auckland; he would later become principal negotiator for Waikato's continuing claims against the Crown arising from the confiscation of their land. She also sent Piki to the Anglican Waikato Diocesan School for Girls in Hamilton. She welcomed the various Christian churches back to the marae, but was particularly close to the ministers and deaconesses of the Methodist church, some of whom were good friends and advisers. From the mid 1930s she worked closely with the new medical officer of health, H. B. Turbott, to tackle high mortality rates from typhoid and tuberculosis. Although the Department of Health had long ago foiled her attempt to provide medical care in a Māori environment in Māhinārangi, she succeeded in the early 1940s in opening a clinic at Tūrangawaewae House (the former Kauhanganui house), where the people felt comfortable. When the Māori Women's Welfare League was formed in 1951, she was elected its first patron.

Te Puea took the most active leadership role in Waikato in her generation. Driven by a vision of restoring the strength of Tainui, she was able to achieve it because of her mana, her tremendous will, the strength she derived from her faith and the guidance of her ancestors, the loyalty she inspired in others, and her remarkable planning and organisational skills. She had a great warmth and generosity, and a wonderful sense of humour, and she communicated easily with people, whatever their background, in Māori or in English. She loved children and was greatly loved by them in turn even though they might be growled at. As she grew older the young ones were in awe of her, watching her direct the affairs of the marae. Often she was very unwell, but nevertheless she worked seven days a week all her adult life.

Although she enjoyed big occasions from time to time, such as balls in Kimikimi with the Te Pou Mangatāwhiri band playing, the old people remember her best in her bag apron and hat, working in the gardens, planting flower beds and raspberry canes, grubbing out blackberry roots, feeding the pigs. She feared the purposelessness of life without work for all the people, just as she feared the impact of drink on family life, and would not let alcohol on the marae. She tried to protect her young people from repeating what she later saw as the mistakes of her own early life: forbidding them to smoke, and marching into hotels to order barmen not to serve drinks to the women, banging her walking stick on the floor. But if the young people sometimes found her strict, they also recognised her deep concern for them all.

Te Puea died at home on 12 October 1952 after a long final illness. Tūmōkai Kātipa lived until 1985. They had no children of their own, but adopted many; their favourite, Pirihira Kātipa, passed away aged only nine in 1939. Te Puea's tangihanga lasted a week and thousands of people made their way to Ngāruawāhia. The prime minister and leader of the opposition attended the funeral; the BBC devoted a broadcast to her memory, and telegrams came from many parts of the world.

Te Puea was recognised as a remarkable leader whose achievements communicated across cultures, and she was hailed as 'the greatest Māori woman of our time'. There was little recognition, though, of the poverty and powerlessness that she had spent her life fighting, and the New Zealand government was still a long way from accepting the statement of Māori autonomy embodied in the Kīngitanga. She would not have liked the constant references to 'Princess' Te Puea; it was a title originally bestowed on her by Pākehā, which she never used herself. The strength of the Kīngitanga at the time of Te Puea's passing is the greatest testimony to her life's work; and on the marae at Ngāruawāhia her unseen presence is felt still.   *Ann Parsonson* with *Te Arikinui Te Ātairangikaahu, Heeni Wharemaru, Mere Taka, Tauhou Mōkena* and *Denese Hēnare*

King, M. *Te Puea*. Auckland, 1977
Obit. *Journal of the Polynesian Society* 61, No 3–4 (Sept.–Dec. 1952): 192–208

Piupiu Te Wherowhero
1886/87?–1937

Ngāti Mahuta woman of mana

Piupiu Te Wherowhero was born, probably in 1886 or 1887, at Whati-whatihoe, Waikato. She was the daughter of Te Wherowhero Tāwhiao of Ngāti Mahuta, the third child and second son of the second Māori King, Tāwhiao Matutaera Pōtatau Te Wherowhero. Her mother was Tamirangi Manahi of Ngāti Tamaoho of Te Kūiti.

Little has been recorded of Piupiu's childhood and upbringing, although she may have attended primary school in Mercer for a time. Like her cousin Te Puea Hērangi, she had an imperious, strong-willed character. She was regarded as a princess in the popular European press, and her status, already high in Māori opinion, was raised still further by the fact that her uncle Mahuta, the third Māori King, delegated the kingship to her father from 1903 until 1910 while he served in the cabinet and on the Legislative Council. Piupiu grew up accustomed to the highest honours and deference within an atmosphere of tapu and religious awe on official occasions. She herself sometimes dressed in the height of fashion. But the Māori kingdom had little means of financial support and through land confiscation its people were often poorer than Māori in other tribal areas. There were times when with Te Puea and the other women she worked in the fields and the kitchens.

Piupiu's father died late in 1911 and Mahuta 11 months later. The new King, Te Rata, suffered from chronic illnesses and was of a retiring disposition. The women of the kāhui ariki (royal family), including Te Marae (Te Rata's mother), Te Puea and Piupiu herself, took leading roles in his reign. It was probably Te Marae who arranged Piupiu's marriage to

Kainuku Vaikai, a kinsman of the Mākea Nui ariki family of Rarotonga. Piupiu made a second marriage to Hīroka Hetet, also known as Hīkaka Hetet, whose parents were Ngātai Ruihi Hetet and Mata Lana, both of Ngāti Maniapoto with Ngāti Tūwharetoa connections. After this she was often known as Piupiu Hetet. There were children of both marriages.

While living among Ngāti Maniapoto, Piupiu came into contact with the Rātana faith. With Tupu Taingākawa and her uncle Haunui Tāwhiao – her closest associate among the family – she was the leader of a strong pocket of Rātana adherents within the King movement. Piupiu presented herself to Rātana as one who could draw Te Rata into the Rātana movement. In September 1922 she was undoubtedly present at Waahi during a disastrous attempt at reconciliation between the two leaders. During this visit the proper protocol was ignored by the Rātana contingent, and the King and his followers considered themselves belittled; a serious division developed between the Rātana and King movements which was never fully to heal in Piupiu's lifetime.

Piupiu went her own way within the King movement. Throughout her life she continued her adherence to Rātana, and with Haunui Tāwhiao, hosted Rātana hui, inviting guests as though she spoke for the movement as a whole. These actions provoked frequent quarrels with Te Puea, who was unsure whether to regard Rātana as a prophet or a charlatan, and was opposed to attempts by Piupiu and the Rātana faction to dominate the King movement.

Like Te Puea, Piupiu saw the landlessness, homelessness, disease and poverty among her people, and took similar steps to combat these evils. Probably in the 1920s, with the encouragement of Te Rata, Piupiu set up a new community, originally called Kēnana (Canaan), on land she owned. Its first houses were made of sacking; chairs were benzine boxes. There was no government or other assistance. Its people struggled to break in land, sow grass and purchase and farm dairy herds, besides raising subsistence food crops such as potatoes, kūmara, pumpkin, marrow and corn. The ground was swampy and liable to flooding, and Piupiu later moved the settlement to higher ground. Unlike Te Puea's, Piupiu's efforts were not covered by the Pākehā press, and all her life she struggled in relative obscurity.

In 1931 Piupiu sponsored Pēpene Eketone, an adherent of Rātana, as the parliamentary candidate for Western Māori; in so doing she was opposing the rest of the kāhui ariki who still favoured Māui Pōmare. In 1928 Rātana himself had favoured his own son, Tokouru, although he had been willing for a period to resign the seat to Te Rata's nominee. This kind of ambivalence probably extended into the 1931 election, and in these circumstances Piupiu was able to support Eketone.

In his last years, 1932 and 1933, Te Rata made an effort to wean Piupiu away from her Rātana allegiance. But Piupiu and Haunui persisted in their own efforts to draw him to the Rātana faith. By 1934 Piupiu was exerting her influence over Te Rata's heir, the new King, Korokī, and was soon involved in a fresh controversy. Haunui and Piupiu had persuaded Korokī to visit Rātana pa instead of accepting an invitation by Ngāti Porou to open their new house at Tokomaru Bay. When a visiting party of Rarotongan nobility was invited to open it instead, Te Puea and other members of the King movement leadership took offence, and a tremendous quarrel ensued among the kāhui ariki. Āpirana Ngata, escorting the Rarotongan party, managed to effect a reconciliation between the King movement factions.

Piupiu Te Wherowhero died, aged 50, on 29 October 1937 at Arapuni. She was survived by Hīkaka Hetet, who died in 1959, and by 10 children. She was buried on Taupiri Mountain on 2 November. Independent, determined and capable, she symbolised a number of struggles: for survival and reconstruction among an impoverished people made helpless through land confiscations; and for recognition of the Rātana faith among the leadership and people of the King movement. She exemplified, also, the strong leadership qualities shown by many women of the Waikato kāhui ariki.   *Angela Ballara*

Henderson, J. M. *Rātana*. Wellington, 1963

King, M. *Te Puea*. Auckland, 1977

Love, R. H. N. 'Policies of frustration: the growth of Māori politics; the Rātana/Labour era'.
   PhD thesis, Victoria University of Wellington, 1977

Worger, W. H. 'Te Puea, the Kīngitanga, and Waikato'. MA thesis, University of Auckland, 1974